P9-DHN-890

JOINING THE JOURNEY

{ a personal adventure into life and liberty }

JOINING THE JOURNEY

{ a personal adventure into life and liberty }

MARY FORSYTHE WITH BETH CLARK

KINGDOM
LIVING
MINISTRIES

Kingdom Living Ministries | PO Box 703685 | Dallas, Texas 75370 | www.kingdomliving.com

JOINING THE JOURNEY
Copyright © 2005 by Kingdom Living Ministries
ISBN: 0-97255683-1-X

All rights reserved. No part of this publication may be reproduced, stored in a retrieval system, or transmitted in any form or by any means—electronic, mechanical, photocopying, recording or otherwise—without prior written permission.

For information contact:
Kingdom Living Ministries
P.O. Box 703685
Dallas, Texas 75370
www.kingdomliving.com

Unless otherwise noted, all Scripture quotations are from the:
NEW KING JAMES VERSION Copyright © 1979, 1980, 1982 by Thomas Nelson, Inc.

Scripture quotations marked NIV are from:
THE HOLY BIBLE, NEW INTERNATIONAL VERSION® Copyright © 1973, 1978, 1984 by International Bible Society. All rights reserved.

Scripture quotations marked NSAB are from:
The New American Standard Bible, © 1960, 1977, 1995 by the Lockman Foundation.

Cover design by Vision Communications | Dallas, Texas
Printed in the United States of America

1 2 3 4 5 6 7   10 09 08 07 06 05

{ contents }

Prepare for Adventure viii
Before You Go ix

Leg 1: The Starting Point

Step 1: Be Honest Where You Are 13
Step 2: Believe that Change Is Possible 16
Step 3: Choose Life at Every Turn 20

Leg 2: The Word

Step 1: Approach the Word as Your Source of Truth 29
Step 2: Take the Word Personally 32
Step 3: Live by the Word... 35

Leg 3: The Holy Spirit

Step 1: Understand that the Holy Spirit Is God 43
Step 2: Be Filled and Refilled with the Holy Spirit 45
Step 3: Enjoy the Ministry of the Holy Spirit 48

Leg 4: Prayer

Step 1: Talk to God 57
Step 2: Listen to God 60
Step 3: Develop a Lifestyle of Prayer 63

Leg 5: The Love of the Father

Step 1: Start at the Cross... 71
Step 2: Remember that God is God 74
Step 3: Know It's for You 78

Leg 6: Your True Identity

Step 1: Know and Believe the Truth 87
Step 2: Accept Yourself 90
Step 3: Embrace God's Design 94

Leg 7: God's Purpose for Your Life

Step 1: Discover Your Destiny 101
Step 2: Know Your Season 104
Step 3: Align Your Life with God's Purpose 108

Leg 8: Heart Attitudes

Step 1: Be Good Ground 117
Step 2: Live from the Inside Out 120
Step 3: Cultivate an Excellent Spirit 123

Leg 9: Spiritual Warfare

Step 1: Realize that You Have an Enemy 131
Step 2: Recognize the Battle 134
Step 3: Use Your Weapons 137

Leg 10: The Mind

Step 1: Victory Begins in the Mind 147
Step 2: Use the "Philippians 4:8 Test" 150
Step 3: Abide in His Love 153

Leg 11: Your Love Walk

Step 1: Fully and Freely Forgive 161
Step 2: Be a Blessing 164
Step 3: Demonstrate the Fruit of the Spirit 167

Leg 12: Continuing the Journey

Step 1: Step Out, but Stay In 175
Step 2: Have Good Traveling Companions 178
Step 3: Walk On 181

Prepare for Adventure!

Around the Kingdom Living Ministries office, one question surfaces more than any other. Whether it comes beautifully penned on elegant stationery, scribbled on paper ripped from a spiral notebook or neatly typed in an e-mail, it is basically the same: "Mary, how can I develop a deeper, more personal relationship with the Lord?" Whether the requests are worded eloquently or clumsily, they all represent a deep hunger in the hearts of people who have read or heard about the transforming work of the Holy Spirit in Mary's life—and what they really want is for Him to touch them and change their lives too.

Mary's response is constant: "Anyone can have a life-changing, life-giving relationship with the Lord. It just takes living by the Word and communing with the Holy Spirit. I can't bring transformation to them, but He can!"

Lives only begin to change as we begin to live by the truth of God's Word and in the power of His Spirit. The Holy Spirit is the only true change agent in the entire universe, and He can transform even the most devastated life into a strong, healthy, radiant reflection of His power and His love.

A changed life is the result of a process—a journey, if you will. Transformation doesn't happen overnight; it takes place little by little, one step at a time. Anyone who is willing to keep putting one foot in front of the other can experience wonderful and radical change. Whether you know it or not, the Holy Spirit is already committed to the journey called "your life." He has awesome things to show you and to give you along the way. He is simply waiting for you to step onto the path of life and wholeness He has already cleared for you, to say "yes" to the process He's already begun in your life. He's just waiting for you to join the journey.

The book you're reading right now is *not* the journey itself; it's simply a travel guide. It will help you know where you're going and how to get there. It will warn you of some potential perils along the way and tell you how to avoid them. In the event that you've ended up in the wrong place by taking the wrong trail, it will direct you back to the path that leads to life and wholeness; and if you've been caught in a trap as you tried to make your journey through life, it will help you break free and begin to walk again. But, best of all, it will help you get acquainted or better acquainted with the Holy Spirit, who is your Leader.

Everybody is walking some sort of a journey and we all make choices as we go. Two of the most important choices each traveler must make are: "Who will I follow?" and "Where will I get my directions?" The Holy Spirit is the best Leader you'll ever know and God's Word is the only reliable set of directions. The Word and the Spirit will take you on the greatest adventure you can imagine!

Beth Clark
Nashville, TN

Before You Go...

As you walk through the pages of this book, you'll come across several different features, all designed to help you make maximum progress on your journey with the Lord. Before you go, I'd like to introduce these features to you and explain how to use them.

Legs of the Journey: On a journey, a "leg" is a specific portion of a longer trip, one section of an entire journey. "Legs" of this journey are equivalent to chapters in other books or workbooks.

"Dear Fellow Traveler" letters: At the beginning of each leg, you will find a letter in which Mary writes to you about the focus of each leg of the journey. She shares some of her own experiences and insights and cheers you on as you walk through that particular subject.

Steps 1, 2 and 3: Because journeys are nothing more than a series of steps, every leg of the journey includes three steps, each focusing on a specific element that relates to the larger topic of the leg. For instance, Leg 7 is entitled, "God's Purpose for Your Life" and includes the following steps: "Discover Your Destiny;" "Know Your Season;" and "Align Your Life with God's Purpose."

Moving Along: On a journey with the Lord, there are certain things you can do to help your progress. By asking you to answer questions, identify issues or struggles in your life and interact with the Holy Spirit, the "Moving Along" features at the end of each step will help you advance to the next step.

Stepping Stones: Stepping stones along a path or across a stream serve as firm places to step or stand while crossing over from one place to the next. Along this journey, your stepping stones will be specific Bible verses or passages that enforce the truths of each step. They also serve as firm foundations on which to stand as these truths are established in your heart.

Mile Markers: Mile Markers are simply bulleted summary points of the key truths and principles found throughout each leg of the journey.

Travel Journal: The Travel Journal is a blank page on which you can record your reflections or notes about what you are learning as you make your way through this book. You may want to use it as a journal in the strict sense of the word; you may want to express yourself by sketching something or pasting in a picture that represents what you have learned or experienced. It's your opportunity to express yourself and your impressions of each leg of your journey in any way you'd like. Be creative! Be free!

P.S.: The P.S. is a short note at the end of each leg, as a follow-up to the "Dear Fellow Traveler" letter at the beginning. It simply serves as a quick, personal word of encouragement from Mary to you.

Unless otherwise noted, all scripture in this book comes from the New King James Version of the Bible. Most of the verses or passages referenced can be found printed within the step in which they are referenced, either in the text or in the Stepping Stones. Bible translations do differ, sometimes significantly, in the way they render certain verses or passages, so if you prefer to use another translation and you find a verse or passage that doesn't seem to make sense, please see the NKJV.

All right, it's time to go; so let's get started!

{ leg 1 of the journey }

THE STARTING POINT

Step 1: Be Honest Where You Are

Step 2: Believe that Change is Possible

Step 3: Choose Life at Every Turn

Dear Fellow Traveler,

How well I remember when my journey with the Lord began in earnest. I had been in prison for about two weeks, when a bureaucratic fluke kept my promised presidential pardon from being signed when the president left office in January 1993. That day, I found out that I would have to serve the entirety of my sentence, and a fellow inmate said to me, "This is a time to praise God. He has a plan for you, Mary—a plan you're totally unaware of—and His plan is good."

The following Saturday morning, I rolled out of my bunk and did something quite out of character for me. In total desperation, I prayed the most honest prayer I had ever uttered: "God, *I* can't do it anymore! Help me!" He has been helping me ever since.

When the Lord first began to lead me down the path of life and liberty, I was just beginning to get acquainted with His Word, but had commited myself to it wholeheartedly because I was so desperate and so devastated. Early every morning, I found privacy in a shower stall, took a seat on the tile floor and asked the Holy Spirit to teach me. In response, He began to show me promises and principles in the Word and to help me see that I had lived most of my life in complete opposition to what I read in the Bible. Almost every verse or passage revealed ways in which I was not living according to the truth of God's Word!

As I discovered the Scriptures, I felt as though I were looking at a map of an unfamiliar shopping mall, struggling to find the dot that indicates, "you are here." It was like being certain I was standing near the north entrance, but finding out I was actually at the south end. For instance, I really thought I was a smart woman, but when I read the book of Proverbs, I discovered that I was living the life of a fool! As the Holy Spirit revealed the Word to me, it was as if the Lord were speaking, "Mary, you are here. You think you are one place—that you've arrived in some areas, or that you are right about some things or that your heart is in a certain condition—but I want to show you the truth about where you really are."

The Holy Spirit knows where you are too, and He wants to lead you down the path of life and liberty. He will reveal the truth about where you are in every area of your life, so you can move toward all He has for you. He will continue to show you where you are throughout your journey with Him because transformation is a process. Wherever you are, you are poised for a great adventure—an adventure into joy and peace, an adventure into intimacy with the Lord, an adventure into freedom and wholeness. This journey, like all journeys, must start somewhere, and it begins with hearing the Holy Spirit say, "You are here." Once you can honestly identify where you are spiritually, you're in a terrific position to begin the journey you were made for. It's going to be great!

God bless you as you go!
Mary

Step 1: Be Honest Where You Are

Search me, O God, and know my heart…Psalm 139:23

When I first began to understand my need to be totally honest and completely transparent with the Lord, I was, frankly, terrified! At first, I hesitated to be so vulnerable with Him because my past had been a panorama of everything from hardheartedness to rebellion to sexual sin to the occult. But then I realized that He knew it all! He had seen it; He had been there when it happened—and He loved me in spite of it. He didn't approve of the things I *did*, but He loved *me*. Even though He knew everything, I could not begin to walk with Him in a deeply personal way until *I* realized the condition I was in. He had to get me to the place where I could identify and admit, "Okay, Lord, I am a wreck. I have been deeply wounded in my life; I have lived more than 30 years with a general sense of rejection and unworthiness; and I have been involved in all sorts of sin." As the Holy Spirit showed me, "you are here," He was not trying to get me to focus on everything I had done wrong; He was trying to help me. I was wounded and didn't know it; I was in bondage and didn't know it. He was trying to heal me and set me free; in order to do that, He had to show me the truth about my condition so I could cooperate with Him. He was not asking me to enumerate all of my shortcomings, struggles, heartaches and sin; He was only asking me to open my heart to the things He revealed, to be honest about them and to ask for His forgiveness and His healing touch.

The Holy Spirit works wonders when we face the truth.

He's asking you, too, to be willing to say, "Lord, I want to see where I really am. Show me the condition of my heart, and reveal the places where my life is not in alignment with Your Word." He's asking you to be honest where you are so He can heal you, set you free and lead you into His great purposes for your life. During this process of discovery, do not let the enemy ensnare you in the trap of condemnation. The Holy Spirit does bring conviction, but He never brings condemnation or guilt; His work always leads to life and brings hope.

When I write to you of being honest where you are, I am encouraging you to ask the Holy Spirit to reveal your attitudes and motives and help you identify your "stuff." The Holy Spirit works wonders when we face the truth—even the things we wish weren't true—but we can't make much progress with Him when we insist upon trying to hide or deny the true conditions of our hearts or trying to make ourselves look better than we are.

Allowing the Holy Spirit to reveal where you are is not a mental exercise; it is simply asking Him to show you where He wants to bring healing, wholeness or strength to you. Don't strive to uncover anything; simply ask Him to show you what truth He wants to reveal about the condition of your heart and the issues with which you struggle. Then wait on Him, and see what He reveals. You will probably need to do this many times during your journey because He reveals truth and brings wholeness in phases, not all at once.

How will you know when the Holy Spirit is showing you something? For instance, you may recall someone's name, have a dream or see a picture or a scene flash across the screen of your mind. He may use circumstances to remind you of a past event or situation in order to help you realize that you are struggling with disappointment, guilt, fear, jealousy, anger or something else. However He speaks to you, don't back away; cooperate with Him. Don't go too fast, just take a few moments, get quiet on the inside and see what He brings to mind and highlights for you.

I really believe, if you will be honest about what is going on inside of you right now, the Holy Spirit will begin to strengthen you, set you free and heal broken places in your heart. The list below includes some of the most common struggles we deal with. If you have experienced, or are experiencing, any of them, I encourage you to put a check mark in the blank beside the ones that apply to you—that's a great first step toward being honest where you are.

___ Disappointment	___ Sin / Disobedience
___ Fear	___ Dishonor toward parents
___ Pride	___ Disrespect for authority
___ Regret	___ Unforgiveness
___ Guilt	___ Insecurity
___ Anger	___ Jealousy
___ Shame	___ Rejection
___ Judgment	___ Bitterness
___ Anxiety	___ Comparison
___ Rebellion	___ Selfishness

There was a time when I would have checked all of the blanks above, so don't be embarrassed or intimidated if you needed to check most or all of them. The more honest you are willing to be about the true condition of your heart, the better position you are in to receive the help and wholeness the Holy Spirit longs to bring you.

Moving Along

1. Using the following simple prayer, or in your own words, say:

"Holy Spirit, would You show me where I am so I can move along on the path of life and liberty? I want to know the truth so I can journey into a deeper relationship with You."

In the space below, write down what He shows you.

_____

_____

_____

_____

_____

_____

2. Psalm 139:23, 24 says, "Search me, O God, and know my heart; test me and know my anxious thoughts. See if there is any offensive way in me, and lead me in the way everlasting" (NIV). If He reveals that there is something offensive in you, how should you respond, according to 1 John 1:9? What does God promise you in this verse?

_____

_____

_____

_____

3. Why does the Holy Spirit want to show you where you are? In other words, what is He trying to accomplish in your life as you are willing to be honest where you are?

_____

_____

_____

_____

4. Before you worked through this step, did you think you were somewhere you weren't? Have you been surprised by anything the Holy Spirit has shown you? What?

_____

_____

Stepping Stones

For the Lord does not see as man sees; for man looks at the
outward appearance, but the Lord looks at the heart.
1 Samuel 16:7

Behold, You desire truth in the inward parts, and in the
hidden part You will make me to know wisdom.
Psalm 51:6

However, when He, the Spirit of truth, has come,
He will guide you into all truth…
John 16:13

Search me, O God, and know my heart; test me and know my
anxious thoughts. See if there is any offensive way in me,
and lead me in the way everlasting.
Psalm 139:23, 24 (NIV)

Step 2: Believe that Change Is Possible

Jesus said to him, "If you can believe, all things are possible to him who believes."
Mark 9:23

In *A Glimpse of Grace*, I wrote that there was a time in my life when I lived "under the ruthless rule of believing that nothing could or would *ever* change." Perhaps you are now where I was then, and you do not really believe change is possible in your life. Maybe you think your pain is too deep, your challenge too steep, your fear too debilitating or your heart too broken. Maybe you feel your problems have become such a tangled web that you can never be free from them. Or, maybe you do not need radical change throughout your entire life, but only have one or two areas in which you have struggled and struggled and cannot seem to overcome. Whatever the case, I understand; I also lived under the dominion of that kind of hopelessness, and I want to tell you that it is a trap of the enemy. One of his most deadly strategies is to deceive us into thinking thoughts like, *Well, I can't really change because everybody in my family has this problem. Or, I'm just this way, and I can't be any different. Things are never going to change for me.*

As you continue on your journey, I urge you to believe and embrace this life-changing truth: *Change is possible; you can be changed; your life can be different.* The power of God's Word and the ministry of the Holy Spirit caused me to believe that change was indeed possible—not only external, behavioral change, but true transformation in my heart. The Lord longs to bring transformation to you too. Your thought patterns *can* change; the way you relate to people *can* change; your financial situation *can* change; your emotional condition *can* change; your marriage *can* change; your family relationships *can* change; your habits *can* change; your attitudes *can* change. Whatever needs to be different in your life, can be— that's what the Holy Spirit does.

> I urge you to believe and embrace this life-changing truth: *Change is possible; you can be changed; your life can be different.*

When the Holy Spirit brings change, He brings improvement. I have seen Him work so many miracles, not only as He has transformed my life, but also as He has changed the lives of people around me. I have seen Him heal shattered hearts, revive dead dreams, restore devastated marriages and break the grip of addictions and torment.

As I write to you about change in your life, I want to specifically address the past. People often feel totally powerless over the past because they cannot go back and change what has happened. True, the circumstances and facts of your past cannot be altered. Whatever has happened, has happened. But the pain of the past can be healed, and its influence in your life can be broken. Whether your pain from the past comes in the form of a disappointment, a failure, rejection, fear, something you're ashamed of or something you haven't been able to overcome, the Holy Spirit can touch and transform you. You see, if the pain of the past is not healed, it can negatively affect the way you think. It can also cause you to make unwise decisions about your future because your choices can be based on pain, fear, or some other work of the enemy. The pain of the past will try to convince you that you cannot change, but that is not true. There is nothing in your past that God cannot redeem for your future. Even if you have made bad choices in the past or suffered the consequences of poor decisions, the Lord loves you and His grace is available to turn your life around. The Holy Spirit works miracles; He is in the business of transformation— and He can change you!

Moving Along

1. In what areas of your life do you really want to see change?

_____

_____

_____

2. Is there anything from your past that has caused you pain, anger or disappointment and is still influencing you today? What is it and how is it influencing you?

_____

_____

_____

_____

3. What do the following verses teach you about breaking free from the pain of your past?

Isaiah 43:18, 19 _____

_____

2 Corinthians 5:17 _____

_____

4. Jesus said in Mark 9:23, "If you can believe, all things are possible to him who believes." Think of a specific area in your life in which you have believed change was impossible. Do you now believe that, with the help of the Holy Spirit, change is possible in that area?

_____

5. If you are longing for change and believing that it is possible by the power of the Holy Spirit, pray the prayer below or a similar one in your own words.

Father, I pray that You would totally destroy the hopelessness in me and release me from the pain of my past. I am asking You to help me see the truth that all things are possible and to help me believe that my life can be different. Thank You for longing to bring change to my life. I open my heart to receive it. In Jesus' name, Amen.

Stepping Stones

Do not remember the former things, nor consider the things
of old. Behold, I will do a new thing, now it shall spring forth;
shall you not know it? I will even make a road in
the wilderness and rivers in the desert.
Isaiah 43:18, 19

"I will give you a new heart and put a new spirit within you;
I will take the heart of stone out of your flesh
and give you a heart of flesh."
Ezekiel 36:26

Therefore, if anyone is in Christ, he is a new creature;
old things have passed away;
behold, all things have become new.
2 Corinthians 5:17

Jesus said to him, "If you can believe,
all things are possible to him who believes."
Mark 9:23

Step 3: Choose Life at Every Turn

I call heaven and earth as witnesses today against you, that I have set before you life and death, blessing and cursing; therefore choose life, that both you and your descendants may live. Deuteronomy 30:19

Once you are in position to be transformed by knowing "you are here," by believing change is possible and by asking the Holy Spirit to help you, the next step is to begin to choose life. In simplest terms, choosing life means aligning everything about you with God's Word and following the Holy Spirit as you make good decisions. By "good decisions," I mean choices that agree with God's Word, incorporate godly wisdom, promote health (spiritual, mental, emotional, relational and physical), lead to maturity and move you forward in God's purposes and plans for your life. Choosing life begins with internal responses and the attitudes of the heart—not with outward expressions or behavior—because when the motives of your heart are right, your actions will follow.

> Every day, circumstances present opportunities for you to choose life or death. Your decisions at those moments will either take you farther down the path of life or make you walk backwards.

For instance, choosing life means choosing forgiveness over resentment, choosing faith over fear, choosing to believe the best instead of the worst about a person, choosing to respond with mercy instead of criticism or judgment and choosing to believe the truth of God's Word over your feelings.

Every day, circumstances present opportunities for you to choose life or death. Your decisions at those moments, even if they seem unimportant or trivial, will either take you farther down the path of life or make you walk backwards. Every choice matters; every choice has consequences; and the journey toward greater intimacy with the Lord is made up of a series of choices for life; it's a process, not an event. The little decisions add up, and together they determine your direction.

Do not let the enemy convince you that any choice is insignificant or that you are ever justified in choosing death (for example, that you have a right to harbor unforgiveness in your heart). Instead, understand that your everyday situations regularly put life and death before you in a multitude of practical ways, such as:

- choosing to walk in integrity at work when you are surrounded by pressure to cut corners or tamper with the truth.
- choosing to be patient, instead of impatient, when you are in a hurry at the grocery store, the person in line ahead of you has an item that needs a price check and the clerk needs to change the register tape.
- choosing to get the rest you need instead of staying up too late to watch a movie.
- choosing to save your money for something you want instead of buying it on credit.
- choosing to help someone in need instead of pursuing your own desires.
- choosing to embrace your individuality instead of falling into the trap of comparison.
- choosing to eat fruits and vegetables instead of foods that are high in saturated fats or sugars.
- choosing to respond with a word of kindness instead of snapping at someone in a stressful situation.

The scenarios listed above are just a few of the many and varied opportunities you may have to choose life as you go about your everyday activities, and the Lord is asking you to participate in the process of transformation by choosing life at every turn.

Moving Along

1. In your own words, what does it mean to choose life?

_____

_____

_____

_____

2. Read Deuteronomy 30:15-20. What are we commanded to do in verse 16, in order to choose life?

_____

_____

According to verse 20, what do we get to do if we choose life? (Fill in the blanks.)

_____ the Lord our God, _____ His voice,

_____ to Him.

3. Can you remember any past situations in which you have not chosen life? What would you have done differently if you had chosen life?

_____

_____

_____

_____

4. How can you begin to choose life in the following areas?

- Spiritual growth _____

  _____

- Health _____

  _____

- Family _____

  _____

- Finances _____

  _____

- Marriage _____

  _____

- Friendships _____

  _____

- Time management _____

  _____

- Job or career _____

  _____

- Entertainment _____

  _____

Stepping Stones

You will show me the path of life;
in Your presence is fullness of joy;
at Your right hand are pleasures forevermore.
Psalm 16:11

Ponder the path of your feet,
and let all your ways be established.
Do not turn to the right or the left;
remove your foot from evil.
Proverbs 4:26, 27

The fear of the Lord leads to life, and he who has it will abide
in satisfaction; he will not be visited with evil.
Proverbs 19:23

I call heaven and earth as witnesses today against you,
that I have set before you life and death,
blessing and cursing; therefore choose life,
that both you and your descendants may live.
Deuteronomy 30:19

Mile Markers

• In order to begin your journey, it really is necessary to allow the Holy Spirit to show you where you are.

• Remember, identifying the areas in which you need change involves allowing the Holy Spirit to speak to you.

• There is nothing the Lord cannot change. In fact, He is longing to bring transformation to every area of your life.

- Remember Mark 9:23, which says that "all things are possible to him who believes." Then ask the Holy Spirit to help you keep believing that change is possible and to help you as you go through changes in your life.

- Everyday circumstances present you with opportunities to choose life or death. All choices have consequences, and no choice is insignificant.

- The journey toward more intimate communion with the Lord is a process, not an event; and it is a process that involves choosing life at every turn.

Travel Journal

Here's your opportunity to take a break, kick back and be creative as you express what the Holy Spirit has taught you about getting started on your journey with Him.

P.S. Remember, every path the Holy Spirit puts you on leads to life!

THE WORD

Step 1: Approach the Word as Your Source of Truth

Step 2: Take the Word Personally

Step 3: Live by the Word

Dear Fellow Traveler,

Few journeys go well when the sojourners do not have a map or a guidebook. Especially in unfamiliar territory, reliable directions are essential. Before I stepped onto the path of life with the Holy Spirit, I consulted all kinds of sources when I needed to know which way to turn—my own intellect, my emotions, financial analyses, news reports, fashion magazines, horoscopes and a variety of other means from which I thought I could find reliable advice. I did everything I knew to do in order to achieve *my* idea of success, but ended up making decisions and taking actions that turned out to be faulty, unstable and of no lasting value.

You too can get your life's directions from a myriad of sources. There are a thousand compasses available, but only God's Word will point you toward "true north." Everything else will lead you down paths of death and destruction. Other avenues might seem to promise satisfaction, prosperity or fun for a season, but the satisfaction will be shallow, the prosperity superficial and the fun fleeting.

I cannot overemphasize the importance of living by the Word of God in every area of your life: relationships, career, finances, marriage, parenting, health and the other everyday situations that call for wisdom. God's Word is the key that releases you from bondage, the balm that heals the wounds and disappointments of your past, the tool that equips you to do what you were created to do. The transforming truths of the Word will change you from the inside out and give you the peace you long for, the direction you seek and the inner strength you need.

Now, perhaps you have never read the Word or have read it in the past and not really grasped it. I want to encourage you not to stumble over what you do not understand and to not get caught up in theological debates. Instead, when you open your Bible, look for truth that speaks to your heart, and be diligent to apply it to your life. Incorporate what the Holy Spirit illuminates to you and, as you do, He will be faithful to increase your understanding and to reveal more and more truth to you.

On the other hand, you may be quite familiar with the Word, and when someone mentions a specific verse or passage, you think, *Oh, I already know what that says*, but I encourage you to keep your heart open to fresh revelation. Hebrews 4:12 tells us that the Word is "living and powerful, and sharper than any two-edged sword," which means it is always capable of speaking to you—no matter how many times you've heard it before.

On this leg of your journey, I pray that your heart will hunger for the Word in an unprecedented way, and that you will make a fresh commitment to turn to it for the guidance you need in every area of your life. The Word works; you'll see.

God bless you as His Word directs your path!
Mary

Step 1: Approach the Word as Your Source of Truth

Sanctify them by Your truth. Your word is truth. John 17:17

Several weeks before I went to prison, I received a letter from a Christian inmate who wrote, essentially, "Whatever you do, get the Word of God in your heart before you arrive here." I didn't know what she meant by, "Get the Word of God in your heart," nor did I understand the urgency with which she wrote. For that reason, I shrugged off the best piece of pre-prison advice I ever received.

Not until I had been there for several weeks did I begin to realize what she meant.

You see, I had run out of options. I had tried everything I knew in order to find peace, healing and true satisfaction—and nothing had worked. In complete desperation, I took a Bible in

> Get the Word into your heart. Believe it for yourself, and do not let circumstances, emotions, people, wrong thinking or experiences persuade you that it is not true or that it will not work for you.

my hands one day, stood in my jail cell and made the commitment that changed my life, as I said to the Lord: "If You will teach me how to live out of this Book, I'll do it—even in a place like this."

Over the weeks and months that followed, the truth of the Word was challenged in my life in a variety of ways. In the battle to believe, my opponents included my circumstances, my past, my own thoughts, my emotions and my flesh. All sorts of faulty mental strongholds (established patterns of thinking) had to be demolished when I decided to approach God's Word as my source of truth. For instance,

- I thought my life was over when I went to prison, but God's Word told me that He had a plan for my life, a plan to give me a hope and a future (see Jeremiah 29:11).
- I struggled so much with self-rejection that I hated to look in the mirror, but God's Word told me that I was fearfully and wonderfully made (see Psalm 139:14).
- I had lived all my life relying on my own intellect, education and good ideas, but God's Word told me that *my* plans could lead to my destruction (see Proverbs 14:12).
- When I was in trouble, I had put my trust in people I thought could help, but God's Word told me that I could not lean on a person or an earthly institution (see Jeremiah 17:5-8).

- I thought what I didn't know wouldn't hurt me, but God's Word told me that I could perish for lack of knowledge (see Hosea 4:6).

No matter what I had to overcome, I was determined to adjust my life to what I read in the Bible. I had made a deliberate decision to believe the Word over my circumstances, over my emotions, over my thoughts, over my *everything*—and I was determined to stick with it, even when it wasn't easy. Now, years after I first chose to believe the Word above all else, I still have to stand against experiences, emotions or thoughts that seek to move me from my absolute assurance that the truth of the Word triumphs over everything.

I have a friend who is a smart businesswoman and an influential leader in her city. She is also a believer, and she reads the Bible regularly. In order to stay sharp in her profession, she reads a number of secular books and magazines, many of which offer counsel that is contrary to the Word. For example, most of these books urge readers to "Look out for yourself. Do everything you can do to get ahead. Fight to win. Be better than the next person." But Philippians 2:3 instructs us to, "Let nothing be done through selfish ambition or conceit, but in lowliness of mind let each esteem others better than himself." If my friend follows the advice of her books, she will be in disobedience to the Word. So instead of treating her secular sources as her final authority in every way, she gleans helpful insights from them, but disregards anything that does not affirm biblical truth. That way, she stays on the cutting edge of her profession while staying safely within the boundaries of biblical wisdom and truth.

I urge you, as that inmate urged me, to get the Word into your heart. Believe it for yourself, and do not let circumstances, emotions, people, wrong thinking or experiences persuade you that it is not true or that it will not work for you. I cannot convince you that the Word is true; you must make that discovery for yourself. But I can tell you, if you will make a commitment to really absorb and obey it, the Word will prove itself to you.

Moving Along

1. Do you approach the Word of God as your source of truth?

_____

_____

2. As you've read through this section, has the Holy Spirit convicted you of any ungodly

sources from which you are seeking truth or direction for your life? What are they and will you stop consulting them?

_____

_____

3. Please read John 8:31, 32. According to these verses, what happens when you know the truth?

_____

_____

4. Are you ready to make a fresh commitment to the Word as the primary compass for your life? If so, say to the Lord, "Lord, teach me how to live by the truth of Your Word in every area of my life, and I'll do it."

Stepping Stones

The entirety of Your word is truth, and every one
of Your righteous judgments endures forever.
Psalm 119:160

The grass withers, the flower fades,
but the word of our God stands forever.
Isaiah 40:8

For this reason we also thank God without ceasing,
because when you received the word of God which you heard
from us, you welcomed it not as the word of men,
but as it is in truth, the word of God,
which also effectively works in you who believe.
1 Thessalonians 2:13

Sanctify them by Your truth. Your word is truth.
John 17:17

Step 2: Take the Word Personally

Your word is a lamp to my feet and a light to my path. Psalm 119:105

One sure way to have transformation in your life is to take God's Word personally. There is so much life, so much peace, so much satisfaction and direction in the Word, but in order to experience and benefit from all that it has to offer, you really must believe and appropriate the Word for yourself.

As I began to learn to take the Word personally, I asked the Holy Spirit every morning, "Would You show me how to practically apply what I'm reading today?" Inevitably, some situation would arise later in the day as an opportunity to do just that. For example, the first time I read 1 Timothy 2:1, 2, which says, "Therefore I exhort first of all that supplications, prayers, intercessions, and giving of thanks be made for all men, for kings and all who are in authority… ," I immediately began to pray for the prison warden, the other administrators, my boss at the warehouse and even the guards. Admittedly, I felt strange knowing I had to pray for them, but I was so hungry to live by the Word that I pushed through my reluctance and did it anyway. (That's called obedience!). Then I shared that scripture with my friends, and the next time we gathered to pray, we all began to intercede for the authorities at the prison, for state and local officials, for national and international leaders.

Nothing will change you like applying the Word to your life, clinging to it when the winds of adversity blow and standing on it against all opposition. In order to help you, or to refresh what you may already know, I'd like to share with you some of the practical lessons I've learned about taking the Word personally.

> Nothing will change you like applying the Word to your life, clinging to it when the winds of adversity blow and standing on it against all opposition.

- Approach the Word with a humble, teachable heart that is willing to make adjustments in order to align with God's truth.
- When you spend time in the Word, ask the Holy Spirit to help you understand what you read, and expect His guidance.
- Believe God's promises are for you. Don't read or listen to the Word thinking that it only applies to someone else.

- Once the Lord shows you a principle in His Word, keep applying it to your life and don't get impatient. Remember, this is a journey, so just keep putting one foot in front of the other.

- Don't compare your spiritual growth and progress with others' (comparison of any kind is unwise).

- Keep a journal of scriptures that speak to you personally.

- Don't just read the Bible; study it. Use reference materials to help you. For example: a Bible study program for your computer, a concordance and/or a Bible dictionary. You might also consider using a good study Bible.

- Read the Word aloud. (When I was in prison, I often read it just loud enough for my own ears to hear it. I still do).

- Meditate on the Word. The word *meditate* means "to mutter" and implies "to ponder." The Word will be established in you as you think about it and repeat it.

- Pray the Word. Use scriptures to pray for yourself and for others. (Chapter 4 will teach you how to do this).

- Share with others the truths that are being made real to you. That way, those truths will be strengthened in your heart.

- Write down individual verses or passages, and put them where you can see them often.

- Memorize Bible verses and Scripture passages.

- Keep a thankful heart while you are in the Word. This will keep you focused on God's love for you and your communication open with Him.

- Look for practical opportunities to apply what you have read or studied in the Word.

- Remember that living by the Word is a process. Results are not always immediately visible, but living by the Word will always bear fruit!

Moving Along

1. In what area(s) of your life have you already begun to take the Word personally? In what area(s) do you need to start applying the Word to your life?

_____

_____

_____

2. How can you practically apply one truth you've learned in the Word to a specific situation in your life?

_____

_____

_____

3. Of the practical lessons in Step 2, which ones will you incorporate in your life in order to help you take the Word personally?

_____

_____

_____

4. With whom can you share a recent truth you've learned in the Word?

_____

_____

Stepping Stones

And the Word became flesh and dwelt among us,
and we beheld His glory, the glory as of the only
begotten of the Father, full of grace and truth.
John 1:14

For the word of God is living and powerful,
and sharper than any two-edged sword, piercing even to the
division of soul and spirit, and of joints and marrow, and is a
discerner of the thoughts and intents of the heart.
Hebrews 4:12

Your word is a lamp to my feet and a light to my path.
Psalm 119:105

Step 3: Live by the Word

But be doers of the word, and not hearers only, deceiving yourselves. James 1:22

Living by the Word is the only way to really live. This kind of living is not only about knowing God's Word, but also about being transformed by it. Transformation is a process that takes time, and it begins with "baby steps." People often ask me, "How did you get started living by the Word?" and I tell them, "It starts with one tiny step, and then another, then another." When I first began my journey toward living by the Word, all I could do was read one verse or one principle and then obey it. Anytime I read something in the Word and realized that my life did not align with it, I knew I had to make the appropriate adjustment—which might have been an attitude shift, a change of behavior, offering an apology or asking forgiveness, changing my perspective or some other response. The adjustments were rarely easy, and the process was an inch-by-inch, moment-by-moment series of choices to obey.

> Living by the Word is a lifestyle, a habit of reading and studying and applying its principles to your daily life, in practical situations.

As you begin to live by the Word, you too can start simply and with small steps. For instance, when you read in the Bible that you are to forgive your enemies, and you know that you are harboring unforgiveness in your heart toward someone, then you need to forgive that person. As another example, when you read a scripture that instructs you care for the poor and needy, then you ask the Holy Spirit what He would have you do—and it may be as simple as writing a check to a homeless shelter or taking a bag of groceries to a food bank. Be determined to integrate into your life every truth the Holy Spirit teaches you as He leads you. He is committed to helping you live by the Word, and He will lead you at the pace that will enable you to do so most successfully.

Sometimes people approach the Word as a shot of medicine or a round of antibiotics. They think that finding a verse to "stand on" in an emergency, posting Scriptures on the refrigerator or reading the Bible in a programmed, legalistic way should bring a quick solution to their problems. But that is not the case; living by the Word is a lifestyle, a habit of reading and studying and applying its principles to your daily life, in practical situations. It is not only using your mind to memorize the words of a meaningful verse, but allowing the truth behind those words to take root in your heart so you can live from it as naturally as a tree lives from its root system. In that way, the Word becomes your life source, and you draw your strategies for daily living from its wisdom and its truth. That's how you live by the Word.

Moving Along

1. What adjustments do you need to make in the time you are spending (or the quality of your time) in the Word or in the way you allow the Word to work in your life?

_____

_____

_____

2. What biblical principle or principles do you know in your head, but have not applied to your life? In other words, in what areas have you been a "hearer only" and not a doer of the Word?

_____

_____

_____

3. If you have been walking with the Lord for more than one year, think back six months ago. Are you expressing more of the Word in your life now than you did then? Tell the Holy Spirit that you want to express more of the Word in your life six months from now than you do today.

_____

_____

4. Have you consulted the Word of God about the following areas of your life?
    ___ Your character (see Psalm 1; Proverbs 10:8, 9; Proverbs 11:3; Proverbs 20:7)
    ___ Your work ethic (see Proverbs 18:9; 2 Thessalonians 3:10)
    ___ Your attitude toward authority (see 2 Peter 2:9, 10; 1 Timothy 2:2)
    ___ Your marriage (see Genesis 2:24; Hebrews 13:4; Ephesians 5:33)

____ Your calling, purpose or destiny (see Proverbs 3:5, 6; Jeremiah 29:11; 1 Peter 2:9)

____ Your thinking (see Isaiah 55:8, 9; Isaiah 26:3; Colossians 3:2)

____ Your emotions (see Proverbs 17:22; Proverbs 12:25; John 14:1a)

____ Your words or speech (see Psalm 19:14; Proverbs 13:3; Proverbs 21:23)

____ Your social relationships (see 1 Corinthians 15:33; Proverbs 17:9; Proverbs 18:24)

____ Your relationship to your church (see Psalm 34:3; Matthew 18:20; Hebrews 10:24, 25)

____ Your personal discipline (see Romans 13:14; Galatians 5:16; 1 Corinthians 9:27)

____ Your acts of service (see Proverbs 22:9; Matthew 6:3, 4; Matthew 25:34-45)

____ Your finances (see Proverbs 3:9, 10; Proverbs 22:9; Malachi 3:10; Luke 14:28, 29)

____ Your health and nutrition (see Romans 12:1; 1 Corinthians 6:19, 20; 1 Corinthians 10:31)

____ Your prayer life (see Psalm 5:2, 3; 1 Thessalonians 5:17; Psalm 55:17)

____ Your relationship with your parents (see Ephesians 6:2, 3; Proverbs 23:24, 25)

____ Your relationship with your children (see Proverbs 22:6; Ephesians 6:4; Colossians 3:21)

____ The way you spend your time (see Deuteronomy 30:19; Ecclesiastes 3:1; Ephesians 5:15-17)

____ Your choices regarding what you watch or listen to (television, movies, music, etc.) (see Psalm 101:2-4; Psalm 119:37; Proverbs 25:28)

____ Your decisions (see Proverbs 1:5; Proverbs 24:3, 4; James 1:5)

Stepping Stones

And these words which I command you today shall be in your heart.
You shall teach them diligently to your children, and shall talk of
them when you sit in your house, when you walk by the way,
when you lie down, and when you rise up.
Deuteronomy 6:6, 7

This Book of the Law shall not depart from your mouth,
but you shall meditate in it day and night, that you may observe to do
according to all that is written in it. For then you will make your
way prosperous, and then you will have good success.
Joshua 1:8

So now, brethren, I commend you to God and to the word of His grace,

which is able to build you up and give you an inheritance

among all those who are sanctified.

Acts 20:32

But be doers of the word, and not hearers only, deceiving yourselves.

For if anyone is a hearer of the word and not a doer,

he is like a man observing his natural face in a mirror;

for he observes himself, goes away,

and immediately forgets what kind of man he was.

But he who looks into the perfect law of liberty and continues in it,

and is not a forgetful hearer but a doer of the work,

this one will be blessed in what he does.

James 1:22-25

Mile Markers

• When you approach the Word, approach it as your source of truth. It is the only compass that always points toward true north, and it will always lead to life.

• Believe the truth of the Word over your circumstances, your emotions, your thoughts, your experiences and other people. Always use the Word as your standard of truth.

• One certain way to true transformation is to believe the Word personally and apply it to your life.

• When you read the Word, ask the Holy Spirit to reveal a truth or a principle you can apply and to give you opportunities to practice what He's shown you.

• Living by the Word is a process; it takes time, and it usually begins with baby steps.

• The Holy Spirit is committed to helping you live by the Word.

Travel Journal

Here's your opportunity to take a break, kick back and be creative as you express what the Holy Spirit has taught you about living by the truth of the Word.

P.S. Living by the Word is the only way to really live!

THE HOLY SPIRIT

Step 1: Understand that the Holy Spirit Is God

Step 2: Be Filled and Refilled with the Holy Spirit

Step 3: Enjoy the Ministry of the Holy Spirit

Dear Fellow Traveler,

One of the lessons the Holy Spirit taught me in prison was that in addition to knowing and living by the Word, I also needed a life-giving relationship with Him. The Word and the Spirit work together. If we are not grounded in the Word and only try to hear subjectively from the Spirit, we can be easily deceived. If we only try to understand and obey the Word, we can become rigid and lifeless. The Holy Spirit causes the Word to spring to life inside of us, and the Word keeps us tethered to the truth as we move in the Spirit. We need both a firm foundation in the Word and a dynamic relationship with the Holy Spirit.

In *A Glimpse of Grace,* I wrote about the dramatic encounter in which I experienced the power of the Holy Spirit—and knew what it was—for the first time. Soon after that, I read about a woman who related to the Holy Spirit as if He were as real and as near to her as any human being. The minute I finished reading, I spoke directly to the Holy Spirit for the first time, saying sheepishly, "H-H-Ho-ly Spirit, if she can know You this way, then I-I-I want to know You this way too."

I felt awkward speaking to Someone I could not see, but the Holy Spirit soon drew me, too, into a friendship more real and more intimate than anything I had ever known. The friendship grew day by day as He taught me to hear His voice and to live by God's Word. Every morning when I opened my Bible, He was there to guide me to the passage I needed to read or study that day, and to help me understand how biblical truth was relevant to my twentieth-century life in a federal prison.

My friendship with the Holy Spirit is still deepening today, and I want to offer you just a brief glimpse into it. We laugh together; we grieve together; and I take counsel with Him in life's big decisions and in the seemingly insignificant choices. He helps me pray; He reveals God's heart for others so that I will know how to comfort, encourage or pray for them; and He makes the heart of the Lord clear as it pertains to my own life. He corrects and convicts me; He gives me wisdom; He enables me to incorporate the promises of God into my life—both in terms of spiritual understanding and practical application. He also relates in ways that seem totally "non-spiritual," and communicates through circumstances, other people, things I see, dreams—through any means He chooses to use to capture my attention and speak to my heart.

A deeper and more vibrant relationship with the Holy Spirit is available to you, and growth comes in relationship with Him as you keep recognizing and yielding to His work in your life.

I encourage you to open your heart as you continue on this journey with the Holy Spirit, and do not be surprised if the He begins to commune with you in ways you've never experienced before.

God bless you as you walk with His Spirit!
Mary

Step 1: Understand that the Holy Spirit Is God

Now the Lord is the Spirit; and where the Spirit of the Lord is, there is liberty.
2 Corinthians 3:17

The first step in developing a truth-based relationship with the Holy Spirit is to recognize and understand that He is God. He is not God's assistant or a junior God; He *is* God. When you are in a growing relationship with the Holy Spirit, you are in a growing relationship with God. The attributes of God are the attributes of the Holy Spirit, and the character and nature of God are the character and nature of the Holy Spirit. When you read the Bible and see what the Father does or what Jesus does, that's what the Holy Spirit does—because He is God.

- Because the Holy Spirit is God, He loves you.
- Because the Holy Spirit is God, He accepts you completely.
- Because the Holy Spirit is God, He provides for you.
- Because the Holy Spirit is God, He comforts you.
- Because the Holy Spirit is God, He rejoices over you.
- Because the Holy Spirit is God, He is faithful to you.
- Because the Holy Spirit is God, He counsels you.
- Because the Holy Spirit is God, He guides you.
- Because the Holy Spirit is God, He disciplines you.
- Because the Holy Spirit is God, He helps you.
- Because the Holy Spirit is God, He teaches you.
- Because the Holy Spirit is God, He's everywhere.

Furthermore, because the Holy Spirit is God, He longs to speak to you, and He will never contradict the Word. Any instruction or guidance you receive from Him is not just a good suggestion. When you hear the voice of the Holy Spirit, it is divine direction; it is from God, and it is to be followed and obeyed. That's good news, because every path He puts you on leads to life.

Before Jesus went to the cross, He said to His disciples, "Nevertheless I tell you the truth. It is to your advantage that I go away; for if I do not go away, the

> The Holy Spirit is your Helper, your Teacher, your Comforter and your Counselor. He wants to lead you into truth and into freedom.

Helper will not come to you; but if I depart, I will send Him to you" (John 16:7). Jesus was telling them that having the Holy Spirit in their midst would be better than having Him with them in person. You see, the Holy Spirit was sent to help us. He does whatever Jesus would do if He were still on earth. Think about it: God the Father is in heaven, Jesus is at His right hand, so which member of the Trinity is with us on earth? The Holy Spirit!

The Holy Spirit is your Helper, your Teacher, your Comforter and your Counselor. He wants to lead you into truth and into freedom. He will convict of sin, but He will not bring condemnation upon you. He will tell you things to come and reveal things your natural eyes cannot see. He will help you understand what God has in store for your life and enable you to receive continual revelation of the Father's love. He is standing by, all the time, just waiting and longing to help you and to give you the guidance you need.

Moving Along

1. What is your perception of the Holy Spirit? Do you relate to Him as God?

_____

_____

2. Are you longing for a deeper relationship with the Holy Spirit? If so, tell Him now, in your own words, that you want to know Him in a deeply personal way, and ask Him to reveal Himself in a fresh way.

_____

3. To read some of what Jesus said about the Holy Spirit, take a moment and read John 14:1-16:15.

4. The scriptures listed below will teach you more about the person of the Holy Spirit. Read them, and in the spaces provided, write what you learn about Him.

- Isaiah 11:2 _____

_____

- Luke 12:12 _____

_____

- Acts 1:8 _____

_____

- Romans 5:5 _____

_____

- Romans 8:26 _____

_____

Stepping Stones

But when the Helper comes, whom I shall send to
you from the Father, the Spirit of truth who proceeds
from the Father, He will testify of Me.
John 15:26

Nevertheless I tell you the truth.
It is to your advantage that I go away; for if I do not go away,
the Helper will not come to you;
but if I depart, I will send Him to you.
John 16:7

Now the Lord is the Spirit;
and where the Spirit of the Lord is, there is liberty.
2 Corinthians 3:17

Step 2: Be Filled and Refilled with the Holy Spirit

But you shall receive power when the Holy Spirit has come upon you. Acts 1:8

Even though I was saved when I was twelve years old and had been in church all of
my life, I had never heard of being filled with the Holy Spirit (which is also called
the baptism of the Holy Spirit), until someone prayed for me soon after I arrived in

prison. When that happened, I was set free from oppression and filled with the most incredible sense of peace, well-being and strength. Over the next weeks and months, I came to realize that I had received an impartation of power I had never known before. I couldn't explain it theologically, but I could not deny its impact. For instance, I recognized a tremendous difference in my prayer life; I was able to understand the Scriptures in a deeply personal way; and I began to sense the Holy Spirit's leading in my everyday circumstances.

The Holy Spirit comes to reside within us when we are born again, but there is more—and it is available to every believer. We simply need to yield to the release of the fullness of His presence and His power in our lives. It's all about His Lordship and our surrender. In other words, we have the Holy Spirit living inside of us in full measure. We don't "get" more of Him; He gets more of us.

When I write to you about the baptism and fullness of the Holy Spirit, I am referring to the diverse, multifaceted manifestations of His presence in our lives. Quite simply, the baptism of the Holy Spirit is asking God to really get involved in every area of your everyday life—and to take control. It is like asking Him to not only come to your house and set up residence, but giving Him permission to open your drawers, rearrange your furniture and move the pictures on your walls!

As you are filled (or refilled) with the Holy Spirit, He will increase your intimacy with Him because He will sharpen your ability to hear His voice, allow you to walk in greater wisdom and revelation, heighten your sensitivity to what He is doing in your life, deepen your ability to commune with Him and open your understanding of spiritual things. He will also empower you to rise above your circumstances, to walk in victory over your flesh, to have fresh vision for your life, to function in the gifts of the Spirit and to make decisions that align with the will and ways of God.

I have seen many wonderful and varied results when people receive the baptism of the Holy Spirit. Some weep; some laugh. Some begin to have spiritual dreams. Some people begin to speak in tongues as soon as they say, "Amen." Some experience a hunger for God's Word like they have never known before. Some feel a

> Quite simply, the baptism of the Holy Spirit is asking God to really get involved in every area of your everyday life—and to take control.

sense of tremendous peace. On the other hand, we receive the baptism of the Holy Spirit by faith, and some people do not "feel" anything at all.

I share this to encourage you, because there is not one "right" response to the baptism of the Holy Spirit. He manifests Himself in different ways with different people. The most important point is that you continue to desire to receive, continue to surrender to Him and continue to be willing to walk by faith.

Moving Along

1. Have you ever been taught that the baptism of the Holy Spirit was a gift for Bible times, but not for today? Have you ever judged or ridiculed the Holy Spirit's work in someone's life or His activity in a service? If so, pray the following prayer or a similar one in your own words.

Father, I ask that You would forgive me for passing judgment against, making fun of, mocking or being offended by manifestations of Your Holy Spirit. Help me to understand and discern His ministry in the days to come. In Jesus' name, Amen.

2. Based on what you've read in this step, what are some of the benefits associated with receiving the baptism of the Holy Spirit?

_____

_____

_____

_____

3. If you have never received the baptism of the Holy Spirit, would you like to have God really get involved in your life in that way?

_____

4. If you would like to receive the baptism of the Holy Spirit, pray the prayer below. I suggest you do this aloud.

Father, I ask You to baptize me with the Holy Spirit. I want everything You have for me, and I surrender my whole life to You. In Jesus' name, Amen.

Stepping Stones

And it shall come to pass afterward that I will pour out My
Spirit on all flesh; your sons and your daughters shall prophesy,
your old men shall dream dreams, your young men shall see
visions. And also on My menservants and on My maidservants
I will pour out My Spirit in those days.
Joel 2:28, 29

I say then: Walk in the Spirit,
and you shall not fulfill the lust of the flesh.
Galatians 5:16

But you shall receive power when the
Holy Spirit has come upon you....
Acts 1:8

Step 3: Enjoy the Ministry of the Holy Spirit

*The grace of the Lord Jesus Christ, and the love of God, and the communion of the
Holy Spirit be with you all. 2 Corinthians 13:14*

The power and the blessings of a relationship with the Holy Spirit become evident
when you experience the fullness of His ministry as a way of life. Ephesians 5:18
reads, in English, "Be filled with the Spirit;" but in the original Greek, the tense
of the verb *be* carries the meaning of continually being filled. So, once you receive
the baptism of the Holy Spirit, you'll need
to continue to be filled and refreshed. Because
you give to others out of the rich treasure of the Spirit within you and because the
pressures of life can cause all of us to "leak," remember to ask the Holy Spirit to refill you
on a regular basis. In addition, keep staying yielded to Him, obeying His leadership and

Enjoy the ministry of the
Holy Spirit in your life.

following Him as He guides you in both spiritual matters and in the practical issues of your life.

Your relationship with the Holy Spirit is a journey, a process. It will unfold over time; there will be seasons of rapid growth and change, and there will be seasons when you feel you are not moving forward at all. Whatever the season, enjoy the ministry of the Holy Spirit in your life, which may include helping you understand the Word as you never have before, putting a passion for prayer within you, causing you to feel a fresh joy as you worship, birthing new desires, filling your heart with thanksgiving or giving you strategies to improve your health or make wise business decisions. Just be on the lookout for the ways He wants to guide and minister to you, then cooperate and enjoy.

What else can you expect after you receive the baptism of the Holy Spirit? Well, you can expect change because part of the Holy Spirit's ministry is to transform us more and more into the image of Jesus. You can also expect some battles, because the baptism of the Holy Spirit does not eliminate your flesh, and your flesh is at war against the things of the Spirit.

Expect, too, that the Holy Spirit will convict you of attitudes or behaviors you need to adjust or of relationships that may need to be altered or redefined. He may ask you to move out of some relationships that do not encourage your walk with Him, but you can also expect to develop some new relationships with other people as the Holy Spirit leads.

Embrace the uniquely personal way the Holy Spirit ministers to you, and don't compare your spiritual experience with someone else's. The Lord has uniquely crafted you, and He works with you in ways that are tailored to your design.

I am convinced that a friendship with the Holy Spirit is vital to your spiritual growth and maturity, and I encourage you to do everything you need to do in order to enjoy His ministry in your life.

Moving Along

1. If you have been filled with the Holy Spirit already, are you continually being filled? If you need to be refilled, pray the prayer below or a similar one in your own words.

> *Holy Spirit, I ask that You would refill me today.*
> *I yield to Your presence and Your power in my life.*
> *In Jesus' name, Amen.*

2. What do the following scriptures teach you about the ministry of the Holy Spirit?

- Isaiah 59:19 _____

_____

- John 6:63 _____

_____

- Romans 8:15, 16 _____

_____

- Romans 15:13 _____

_____

- 1 Corinthians 2:9-12 _____

_____

3. In what ways are you enjoying the ministry of the Holy Spirit in your life?

_____

_____

_____

_____

4. As you've read this step, have you become aware of any changes you can make in order to better cooperate with what the Holy Spirit is doing in your life and to more fully enjoy His ministry? What are they?

_____

_____

_____

_____

Stepping Stones

"Not by might nor by power, but by My Spirit,"
says the Lord of Hosts.
Zechariah 4:6

If you then, being evil, know how to give
good gifts to your children,
how much more will your heavenly Father
give the Holy Spirit to those who ask Him!
Luke 11:13

And I will pray the Father, and He will give you another
Helper, that He may abide with you forever—
the Spirit of truth, whom the world cannot receive,
because it neither sees Him nor knows Him;
but you know Him, for He dwells with you and will be in you.
John 14:16, 17

The grace of the Lord Jesus Christ, and the love of God,
and the communion of the Holy Spirit be with you all.
2 Corinthians 13:14

Mile Markers

• The Holy Spirit is God. He is not a "junior" God. The full measure and stature of the Godhead resides in Him, and He operates in the full authority of God.

• Whatever you read in the Bible about the personality or actions of God the Father and of Jesus, the same is true about the Holy Spirit.

• Remember, the Father is in heaven, Jesus is at His right hand and the Holy Spirit is on earth.

- The baptism of the Holy Spirit will make an enormous difference in your life—both spiritually and in your practical everyday existence.

- Continue to be filled and refilled with the Holy Spirit.

- The Holy Spirit longs for you to be filled with His presence and His power. He will help you and work with you in ways that are unique and perfect for you.

- The ministry of the Holy Spirit will change your life, so receive and enjoy it.

Travel Journal

Here's your opportunity to take a break, kick back and be creative as you express what the Holy Spirit has taught you about Himself and your growing relationship with Him.

P.S. May the communion of the Holy Spirit be with you!

PRAYER

Step 1: Talk to God

Step 2: Listen to God

Step 3: Develop a Lifestyle of Prayer

Dear Fellow Traveler,

God is great. God is good. Let us thank Him for our food. Ah-men. I suppose that was the very first prayer I ever prayed, and I said it before every meal around my parents' kitchen table, beginning as soon as I could put words together in a sentence. When I was twelve years old, I prayed the prayer of salvation and entered into a relationship with Jesus. But then I didn't speak to Him much for more than twenty years.

Then I got in trouble—big trouble. When I ended up in prison, I quickly discovered that the Lord was the only one to whom I could turn. I realized that if I really wanted Him to help me, I would have to talk to Him and keep talking; I would have to listen to Him and keep listening. To be honest with you, in the earliest days of my prayer life, I thought, *This is weird. You mean, I'm supposed to talk to Someone I can't see and believe that He's listening to me—and that it makes any difference?*

Because the Holy Spirit heard my thought, He spoke to me and helped me understand that prayer is a vibrant, heart-to-heart exchange between God and an individual. It is the way you enter into and cooperate with God's desire to release power and bring change; it is the way you share your heart with Him and hear His heart for a person or a situation; and it is a means by which you join Him in His plans for your life, the lives of those you love and the things that are important to you.

Even after He gave me those insights, I still found prayer to be a battle at times. I still wondered if it really could change anything. But I later understood that part of my faith journey included overcoming the struggle to believe that prayer does make a difference. As my relationship with the Holy Spirit developed, prayer sprang to life within me, and I was drawn to pray at every opportunity—when I needed victory, when I was thankful, when I needed wisdom and guidance, and when I needed the intimate and dynamic communication that only exists through prayer.

When I read in James 5:16 that "the effective, fervent prayer of a righteous man avails much," I realized that it is the process of ongoing, regular prayer that will indeed "avail much" and bring change. Sometimes you will see immediate answers to your prayers, and at other times you may have to labor in prayer over a particular situation before you see the Lord respond. Whatever the case, prayer *is* effective! It includes some of the most exciting, challenging conversations and some of the most comforting, tender moments you can imagine—all because you are interacting with the Lord.

In the process of prayer, you will see change, but you will also be changed. Prayer is a rich journey that will lead you into ever-increasing intimacy with the Lord, change your perspective on circumstances and situations and give you an invisible source of strength and wisdom in your everyday life. I am still discovering the wonders of prayer and, as my relationship with the Holy Spirit grows, my ability to express my heart in prayer increases. We're all on the path of effective prayer together!

God bless you as you pray!
Mary

Step 1: Talk to God

I will pray with the spirit, and I will also pray with the understanding.
1 Corinthians 14:15

In this step, I'd like to focus on three specific ways you can talk to the Lord. First, I want to encourage you to talk to Him as naturally and easily as you would speak to a friend over lunch. Talk to Him with the same rhythm, the same intonations, even the same expressions that are part of your everyday conversation. When you pray, you are sharing yourself with the Lord, and you will do that best using your unique expressions and style of communication.

It's okay to laugh with Him, tell Him why you are frustrated or use your tears to communicate when words fail you. Be really honest with the Lord (He knows it all anyway) and decide that no subject will be off limits. The Lord is so interested in the things that concern you; He wants to be deeply involved in your life, so go ahead and tell Him. In the midst of telling Him your "stuff," don't forget to also tell Him how thankful you are, how much you appreciate His grace, how much you love Him and long to grow in your relationship with Him. Yes, you'll have needs and things you just want to process with God in prayer, but you will always have something to be thankful for, so say "thanks"—and say it often.

> The Lord is so interested in the things that concern you; He wants to be deeply involved in your life.

Second, did you know that you can talk to God using His words? Using the Bible to pray is one way to know that you are praying in accordance with God's will and in alignment with His Word. I really began my prayer life by praying the Word, using the prayer in Ephesians 3:16-21. You might want to stop and read that prayer in the Bible first and then read the example below, which will help you know how to personalize Scripture prayers and pray them for yourself and those you love.

Father, I pray that You would grant me, according to the riches of Your glory, to be strengthened with might through Your Spirit in my inner man, that Christ may dwell in my heart through faith; that I, being rooted and grounded in love, may be able to comprehend with all the saints what is the width and length and depth and height—to know the love of Christ which passes knowledge; that I may be filled with all the fullness of God. Now to You who are able to do exceedingly abundantly above all that I ask or think, according to the power that works in me, to You be glory in the church by Christ Jesus to all generations, forever and ever. Amen.

To pray the Word, here's what you do. Find a scripture and then make it personal by inserting your own name or the name of the person for whom you are praying. I'll list several scriptures below to help you get started.

- Psalm 103:1-5
- Proverbs 3:5, 6
- Isaiah 42:16
- Lamentations 3:21-25
- Romans 15:13
- Philippians 1:6
- 2 Thessalonians 1:11, 12

The third way to talk to God is to speak to Him in a prayer language. This language is sometimes referred to as "tongues," and it is a spiritual language that bypasses the natural understanding. If you have received the baptism of the Holy Spirit, you may have received a prayer language. It may not consist of more than one or two syllables or one or two words, but if you will be faithful to pray them over and over, more will be released to you.

When I first began praying in my prayer language, I felt so awkward. My mind kept telling me I was crazy, but somehow, I knew that I had to press through the opposition and do it anyway. One time, when I felt especially challenged, the Holy Spirit showed me a vision of a thick jungle with growth so dense that a person could not walk through it. He showed me that praying in a prayer language is like using a machete to cut through the jungle with ease. It makes a way for God's will to be brought forth, His desires to become reality and His power to be released into people's circumstances.

> Praying in a prayer language makes a way for God's will to be brought forth, His desires to become reality and His power to be released into people's circumstances.

One time, I instinctively knew how to respond to a difficult situation, and when I thanked the Holy Spirit for helping me, He revealed that I had already prayed about that situation, but had done so in my prayer language. Praying in a prayer language will build you up on the inside, help you pray in agreement with God's will and set you free from the influence of your own thoughts. Praying in a prayer language is such an effective way to pray, and I hope you'll discover the power and intimacy it will bring to your communion with the Holy Spirit.

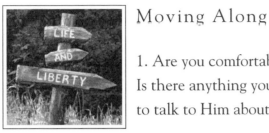 ## Moving Along

1. Are you comfortable talking to God and really sharing your heart? Is there anything you have declared "off limits" or that you are afraid to talk to Him about? What is it?

_____

_____

_____

2. List five things for which you are thankful. Then express your gratitude to the Lord in prayer.

_____

_____

_____

_____

_____

3. How can you use a scripture to pray about a specific person or situation? For instance, for whom can you pray Ephesians 3:18, 19?

_____

_____

4. Do you pray in a prayer language? If so, would you begin to do it more often? As you know, the benefits are tremendous! If not, ask the Lord to give you a prayer language.

_____

Stepping Stones

Lord, I cry out to You; make haste to me!
Give ear to my voice when I cry to You.
Let my prayer be set before You as incense,
the lifting up of my hands as the evening sacrifice.

Psalm 141:1, 2

But you, beloved, building yourselves up on your most
holy faith, praying in the Holy Spirit,
keep yourselves in the love of God, looking for the mercy of
our Lord Jesus Christ unto eternal life.

Jude 20, 21

He who speaks in a tongue edifies himself....

1 Corinthians 14:4

What is the conclusion then? I will pray with the spirit,
and I will also pray with the understanding.

1 Corinthians 14:15

Step 2: Listen to God

And He said to them, "He who has ears to hear, let him hear!" Mark 4:9

The Lord is always longing to speak to you, and prayer involves not only talking to Him, but also listening to Him. Being able to hear God's voice clearly will significantly enrich your prayer life. He wants to share His heart with you, offer insight and give you direction in everything that concerns you.

Just as you have ears on your physical body, you also have spiritual ears. Your natural ears are one of the primary vehicles through which you gain information, get direction and receive what other people are saying to you. Without some means of hearing and receiving from others, true communication is impossible. Your spiritual ears are the "ears of your heart," the ears that can hear God's "still, small voice."

Hearing God is not as mystical as you might think. First and foremost, He speaks through His Word, and when you read the Bible, your spiritual ears can hear His voice. The Lord will never contradict the Word, but it is not His only means of communication. He will also speak to you in ways you can only hear in your heart, and He will speak in a variety of practical ways.

For example, let's say He wants to help you grow in your prayer life. He might speak to you about that using some of the following situations. You may stop at a stoplight and see someone who reminds you of a friend in the car next to you. The Holy Spirit could be speaking: He may be jogging your memory in order to prompt you to pray for your friend. Or, perhaps He wants you to pray for a specific nation or group of people. In such an instance, He may inspire you to pray by causing your heart to be burdened and your compassion to be stirred when you see a scene from a foreign country on the evening news. You might even wake up one morning and remember a dream that provokes you to pray for a person or a situation; He was speaking

> Your spiritual ears are the "ears of your heart," the ears that can hear God's "still, small voice."

to you during the night. Or, you might just keep thinking about someone, and for no apparent reason, you can't get him or her off of your mind. That inability to "shake" the person may be the Holy Spirit's way of asking you to pray.

The Holy Spirit can also use a combination of methods to communicate. For example, my friend Betty recently shared with me a dream in which she rescued a person who had wronged her several years earlier. The next morning, she awakened with the idea to give that person a specific amount of money. She then randomly opened her Bible to Proverbs 25:21, 22, which confirmed her idea.

Later that day, she said, "Mary, I think the Lord is asking me to give some money to So-and-so." All I said was, "That reminds me of Proverbs 25:21, 22—the Bible verse that talks about heaping coals of fire on your enemy's head." Betty looked at me in amazement because she had not told me she felt that very verse confirmed what the Lord was speaking to her. I explained to Betty that the biblical meaning of "heaping coals of fire on your enemy's head" is not to exact revenge, but to cause a person's heart to soften and melt as fire will cause even iron to become soft and malleable. Through the combination of a dream, an idea, a Bible verse, consultation with someone she trusted and understanding of the Word, Betty was able to hear God's voice and begin preparing to obey Him.

The Holy Spirit really wants you to be able to hear Him. He is not trying to make it difficult for you. He will speak to you in ways that you can understand, so I encourage you to ask Him right now to open your spiritual ears to His voice. The more you get to know the Holy Spirit, learn to get quiet on the inside, spend time in the Word and in prayer, the more you will be able to recognize His voice and hear what He is saying to you.

Moving Along

1. Have you ever thought you heard God's voice and then been disappointed when you realized you hadn't heard Him after all? Please describe that situation and then ask the Holy Spirit to heal your heart of that past disappointment so you can hear Him in the future. It's time to start listening again!

_____

_____

2. List three scriptures through which the Lord has spoken to you in the past. (Putting a date beside these scriptures in your Bible is a good way to remember what and when the Lord has spoken to you through His Word).

_____

_____

_____

3. According to what you've learned in Step 2, what are some of the various ways the Lord may speak to you? Can you think of some additional ways He could speak? What are they?

_____

_____

_____

4. Get quiet on the inside for a moment; ask the Lord to open your spiritual ears and communicate something to your heart. You can use the following prayer, or pray a similar one in your own words:

> _Lord, help me to hear Your voice more clearly and to recognize when You are speaking to my heart. In Jesus' name, Amen._

Stepping Stones

Then He opens the ears of men, and seals their instruction.

Job 33:16

Apply your heart to instruction,

and your ears to words of knowledge.

Proverbs 23:12

Your ears shall hear a word behind you, saying,

"This is the way, walk in it," whenever you turn to the

right hand or whenever you turn to the left.

Isaiah 30:21

And He said to them, "He who has ears to hear, let him hear!"

Mark 4:9

Step 3: Develop a Lifestyle of Prayer

Pray without ceasing.... 1 Thessalonians 5:17

There are times that should be set aside for the specific purpose of prayer, but there is also a lifestyle of prayer that involves tuning into heaven throughout the day. It is living with an awareness of the nearness of the Holy Spirit and with a conscious desire to allow Him to influence your thoughts, words and actions in every circumstance. So many times, I think I know best how to respond to a person or a situation, but over the years, I've had to learn to "check in" with the Holy Spirit to see if He wants to direct me some other way. I don't do this in such a way that other people know I'm praying; it all takes place on a heart level and enables me to be "supernaturally natural."

To "pray without ceasing" is to cultivate a lifestyle of prayer. It is a way of life in which you acknowledge and understand that you are totally dependent on the Lord and that you need and want Him to intervene in your practical everyday life.

To "pray without ceasing" is to cultivate a lifestyle of prayer. It is not an event or an activity, but a way of life in which you acknowledge and understand that you are totally dependent on the Lord and that you need and want Him to intervene in your practical everyday life. A lifestyle of prayer requires that you learn to pray without having to speak aloud or to assume a certain posture. It means communicating with the Holy Spirit as you do the dishes, drive to work, watch a soccer game, get a haircut or ride an elevator. Praying without ceasing is inviting the Lord into your heart and your life, moment by moment, day by day.

Every prayer you pray does not need to be a major production. You can pray for people you've never met and for situations you know nothing about, just by mentioning them to the Lord. There is so much power in a simple prayer. Think about the examples listed below.

- There is so much power released when you see a needy person, and whisper in your heart, "Oh, Lord, please help that person."
- There is so much power when you read a tragic story in the newspaper and ask Him to comfort the people affected by it.
- When you drive by a hospital, you can release power by simply saying, "Lord, let Your healing and Your life flow through each hospital room."
- When you hear a news story about your local prison, you can affect lives by saying, "Lord, please reveal Yourself to the inmates in that prison."
- When you are walking or riding your bicycle in your neighborhood, you can release power by saying in your heart, "Lord, bless the people who live in the red brick house. Lord, bless the people with the two children, who live on the corner."
- When you walk into your workplace, you can release power by praying in your heart for those in authority over you and for your coworkers.
- When you receive a card or an e-mail from a friend sharing good news, you can say, "Thank you, Lord. Bless my friend. I rejoice with her in this good news."
- You can release so much power when you sit on an airplane and say a simple prayer, asking the Lord to save those who are lost.

See? Your life is filled with opportunities to pray. I hope you'll take them. You really can pray without ceasing!

Moving Along

1. When have you doubted that prayer really makes a difference? Take a moment now to repent for that, and then ask the Lord to restore your faith in simple prayers.

_____

_____

2. What are three common, everyday activities during which you can begin to practice praying without ceasing?

_____

_____

_____

3. What keeps you from a lifestyle of prayer?

____ television

____ telephone

____ excessive busyness or overcommitment

____ the computer

____ entertainment

____ weariness, laziness or fatigue

____ inability to focus

____ lack of discipline

____ anger or unforgiveness

____ doubt or unbelief

____ hard-heartedness

Ask the Holy Spirit to help you overcome these distractions.

4. In addition to the examples given in Step 3, what other situations can you think of in which you can release power through simple prayers?

_____

_____

Stepping Stones

Evening and morning and at noon I will pray,
and cry aloud, and He shall hear my voice.
Psalm 55:17

Rejoicing in hope, patient in tribulation,
continuing steadfastly in prayer. . . .
Romans 12:12

Pray without ceasing.
1 Thessalonians 5:17

Mile Markers

• Talk to the Lord as easily as you would talk to a friend. Use the language and expressions that are comfortable for you.

• Decide that you will be totally open and honest with the Lord when you talk to Him. Hold nothing back.

• Three ways to talk to God are: by using your own words, by praying the Scriptures and by praying in a prayer language.

• Just as you have natural ears, you also have spiritual ears. You hear the Lord through your spiritual ears.

• The Lord speaks in a variety of ways. It is not mystical; most of the time it is quite practical.

• Incorporate communication with the Holy Spirit into the everyday activities of your life.

• Don't forget to exercise the power of simple prayer in your everyday life.

Travel Journal

Here's your opportunity to take a break, kick back and be creative as you express what the Holy Spirit has taught you about prayer.

P.S. Look out! Opportunities to pray are on their way!

THE LOVE OF THE FATHER

Step 1: Start at the Cross

Step 2: Remember that God Is God

Step 3: Know It's for You

Dear Fellow Traveler,

There is something the Holy Spirit can reveal to you that brings hope, joy, satisfaction and inner strength in a way that *nothing* else does. It is more powerful than any circumstance you will ever find yourself up against. It is there for you in the midst of your darkest night and on your best days; it's there when everything is falling apart and when everything finally comes together. It will bring stability to your life, strengthen you in every situation and help you discern and overcome the work of the enemy. *What is it?* you wonder. It's the enormous, inexpressible, endless, unconditional love of the Father.

I so desire for you to know His love more and more in your life and for it to be the foundation from which you live. Having a working, biblical knowledge of God's love is really not enough; you need to have a revelation of it—to really grasp it in your heart as the Holy Spirit reveals it. Head knowledge will not change your life, but heart comprehension will.

The enemy has probably dealt with you the way he has most people—doing everything he can to prevent you from having a heart revelation of the love of the Father. He may have told you that God loves everyone else, but He doesn't really love you. He may have planted thoughts in your mind that you are not good enough to merit God's love or that you have not performed well enough to earn it. Those are all lies; the enemy attacks you with them because he knows how much power you will wield in the spiritual realm and how much peace and stability you'll have in your life once the issue of God's love begins to be established deep within your heart.

One morning, while I was in prison, I opened my Bible to Ephesians 3. I could hardly believe the words I read. They were bursting with life and hope, and they so precisely communicated what my heart really longed for—an ability to grasp God's incredible love for me. As I prayed that passage over a period of time, I saw an amazing transformation begin to take place inside of me. I'm convinced that beginning to understand and receive God's love built a firm foundation from which I could learn and apply other spiritual truths.

After my release from prison, someone asked what impacted me most of all during my incarceration. I could summarize it in a short, familiar sentence: "Jesus loves me, this I know."

Walking deeper into the knowledge of the Father's love for you is the greatest journey you will ever make. The security and satisfaction that come from knowing you are loved will change your life. The Father's love will empower you, encourage you and set you free. It never runs out, and you will never exhaust all that He has for you. Discovering His awesome love in ever-increasing measure is one of the greatest experiences you'll ever have. Jesus loves you; He really does. *This* I know.

God bless you as He reveals His awesome love!
Mary

Step 1: Start at the Cross

For the message of the cross is foolishness to those who are perishing, but to us who are being saved it is the power of God. 1 Corinthians 1:18

Soon after I was released from prison, I began attending a church in which a large, rugged, wooden cross hung behind the platform. Every Sunday, I wore my nicest dress and an invisible cloak of shame that had shrouded me most of my life and gotten heavier and heavier as the years went by. It made me feel unclean, unapproachable, unworthy and unlovable; it kept me from being able to relate to people and, after prison, it kept my head glued to my chest in every social situation from the grocery store to my job to a Christmas party. It weighed so heavily upon me and seemed to cover me with such filth that I wondered if I would ever be able to crawl out from under it.

Week after week, I sat in my seat during the church service and stared at the cross on the wall. I knew that I was tormented by shame and burdened by its weight, but I also knew that Jesus had carried my shame on the cross. For months, I fixed my gaze upon the cross and kept thinking, *I am not going to take this shame. Jesus bore this for me; it is not mine to carry.* Everywhere I went, I remembered the cross, and I meditated on everything it meant. Eventually, there came a time when I realized that the cross had done a work in me, and I was no longer ashamed. It was a battle; it was a process; but victory came.

> Victory can always be found at the cross, where God's supreme expression of love for you took place more than two thousand years ago.

Victory can always be found at the cross, where God's supreme expression of love for you took place more than two thousand years ago. That's right, the Lord demonstrated His ultimate love long before you were ever born, long before your mother and your father ever met, long before even your great-great-great-grandparents ever caught each other's eye. In God's wisdom, foresight and affection for you, He sent Jesus to die an excruciating death so that you—yes, you, right now—could be free and forgiven, completely righteous and able to approach Him without fear or shame.

In order to better understand the love of the Father, we need to look at the exchange that happened at the cross, when Jesus took all the punishment that was due you as a sinner and freely gave you, instead, all the good that He deserved. At the cross, He disarmed the forces of evil (see Colossians 2:15), and at the cross, you were given victory not only over death, but also over the works of the enemy in your life today. Take a look at the chart below, which lists some of the aspects of the exchange of the cross.

Jesus took your:	Jesus gave you:	Scripture Reference
sin	righteousness	2 Corinthians 5:21
curse	blessings	Galatians 3:13, 14
rejection	acceptance	Ephesians 1:6
shame	glory	Hebrews 12:2
turmoil	peace	Colossians 1:19, 20
despair	hope	1 Peter 1:3
bondage	freedom	Galatians 5:1
darkness	light	Colossians 1:13
sickness	health	1 Peter 2:24
poverty	abundance	2 Corinthians 8:9
death	life	Romans 6:4, 5

To this day, I love to "stare" at the cross and allow the revelation of what happened there to transform me. It continues to bring me hope, liberty and a deeper revelation of the Father's love. I believe it will do the same for you!

Moving Along

1. In your own words, what does the cross mean to you? How can you see God's love expressed toward you through Jesus' death on the cross?

_____

_____

_____

_____

2. In the chart on the opposite page, which of the words in the left-hand column have been particular struggles for you? I encourage you to memorize and meditate on the scripture references associated with them.

_____

_____

_____

3. Has it ever occurred to you that Jesus' finished work on the cross defeated the forces of evil in your life today? What are those "forces of evil" (i.e., challenges, struggles or bondages)? If you have not realized that Jesus' death defeated these things, would you pray and ask the Holy Spirit to give you a revelation of the cross so that you can enforce Jesus' victory in your everyday life?

_____

_____

_____

Stepping Stones

But God demonstrates His own love toward us,
in that while we were yet sinners, Christ died for us.
Romans 5:8

For I determined not to know anything among you
except Jesus Christ and Him crucified.
1 Corinthians 2:2

For the message of the cross is foolishness
to those who are perishing,
but to us who are being saved it is the power of God.
1 Corinthians 1:18

I have been crucified with Christ;
it is no longer I who live,
but Christ lives in me;
and the life which I now live in the flesh
I live by faith in the Son of God,
who loved me and gave Himself for me.

Galatians 2:20

Step 2: Remember that God Is God

God is not a man, that He should lie, nor a son of man, that He should repent. Has He said, and will He not do? Or has He spoken, and will He not make it good?"
Numbers 23:19

You may wonder why I would encourage you to "remember that God is God" in a chapter in which we are exploring His love for you. The reason is that I have known so many people who—even after reading the Bible, praying and going to church for years—struggle to see God's nature and His love clearly because they have transferred the failures, or perceived failures, of parents or primary caregivers onto the Lord. This almost always happens unintentionally, but it does great damage to a person's relationship with the Lord because it prevents him or her from perceiving and relating to the Lord as He really is.

If you really want to know who God is, look in the Word. Nothing reveals Him more accurately than what He has spoken about Himself.

God's perfect design is for parents or primary caregivers to reflect His nature, but because we live in a fallen world and the enemy seeks to twist our thinking about God in every possible way, those people often fail to represent the Lord accurately—or at least we think they do. For instance, if you perceive a parent or caregiver to be temperamental or moody, you may be inclined to think God is unpredictable. If one of them disappoints you, you may tend to think the Lord will let you down too. The chart below may help you recognize how your ideas about the Lord have been shaped by your perceptions of your parent or caregiver.

If Your Parent or Caregiver...	You May See God as...
• was legalistic or a harsh disciplinarian	• angry, authoritarian, impersonal, demanding
• was a perfectionist, set extremely high goals, offered little praise or affirmation	• never satisfied, always disappointed and upset with you
• showed little or no affection	• impersonal, distant
• was critical or verbally abusive	• angry or putting up with people without really loving them
• was a workaholic whose focus was outside of the home and away from the children	• detached and uncaring, distracted and uninterested in you
• was abusive or domineering	• ruling by intimidation; someone you have to obey, but don't really trust
• was moody or temperamental	• unpredictable, loving you one day and being angry or threatening the next
• was sinful, immoral or had a low standard of discipline and behavior	• a pushover, gracious to the point of not enforcing what He says
• smothered you, doted on you, spoiled you and never said no	• existing only for you and your needs and desires, needing to conform to your idea of who He should be
• had favorite children or compared you with siblings and others	• playing favorites, loving "good people" more than sinners, loving you based on your performance
• made promises and broke them or gave warnings and didn't follow through	• unreliable and unfaithful, not bound by His Word
• was hypocritical or lived one way at home and another way in public	• impotent and irrelevant, unable to relate to your life, wanting you to reserve religion for social and special purposes

(adapted from *Freedom from Your Past* by Jimmy Evans and Ann Billington, copyright © 1994)

As the Holy Spirit begins to lead you into a true understanding of who God is and shows you how your perceptions of parents or caregivers have affected your concept of God, I want to caution you against being judgmental or angry. The enemy would love to lure you into the traps of judgment, anger or unforgiveness as you are being set free from a distorted image of God. When you realize where people have failed to represent God accurately, walk in mercy, forgive them and ask the Lord to bless them and to heal your heart from any wounds that may have resulted from your interaction with them.

If you really want to know who God is, look in the Word. Nothing reveals Him more accurately than what He has spoken about Himself. In addition, I encourage you to ask and allow the Holy Spirit to reveal the Father and His love to you. No human being can ever display all of the multifaceted love and perfection of God, but the Lord does send people into our lives to show us aspects of Himself. With the help of the Holy Spirit, we can see past the failures of anyone who holds or has held a position of influence in our lives and begin to see the Lord as He is and receive the lavish love He offers.

Moving Along

1. Look over the chart on the previous page. Can you see where you have allowed a person's weakness to influence the way you perceive or relate to the Lord? In order to begin to see God clearly and receive His love for you, it is necessary for you to forgive that person. Use your own words or the prayer below.

> *Father, I choose to forgive (<u>insert name</u>) for the times (<u>he/she/they</u>) did not reflect Your character, and I bless them. Lord, help me to see You more clearly. In Jesus' name, Amen.*

2. Are you a parent or primary caregiver? In what ways are you reflecting God's character to those who look up to you? What changes do you need to make in order to better reveal His nature?

_____

_____

_____

3. Read 1 Corinthians 13:4-8. Every place you see the word *love*, replace it with *God*. See what you learn about His love for you. Write down the qualities of His love as they are revealed in these verses.

_____

_____

_____

_____

Stepping Stones

Give thanks to the Lord for he is good;
his love endures forever.
Psalm 118:1 (NIV)

But God, who is rich in mercy,
because of His great love with which He loved us,
even when we were dead in trespasses,
made us alive together with Christ
(by grace you have been saved)....
Ephesians 2:4, 5

God is love.
1 John 4:8

God is not a man, that He should lie,
nor a son of man, that He should repent.
Has He said, and will He not do?
Or has He spoken, and will He not make it good?
Numbers 23:19

Step 3: Know It's for You

Now hope does not disappoint, because the love of God has been poured out in our hearts by the Holy Spirit who was given to us. Romans 5:5

It is one thing to know *about* God's love; it's another thing altogether to know His love is especially for you and to have a deep personal revelation of it in your heart. In order to help you progress on your journey into a greater revelation of the Father's love for you, I'd like to ask you some questions:

• Do you really believe God loves you?
• Are you confident in His affections toward you?
• Are you convinced beyond a shadow of a doubt that He is on your side?
• Are you resting in His love for you, knowing that it will never change?
• Do you know that God rejoices over you? Can you hear Him singing?
• Are you living in the assurance that there is absolutely nothing you can do to change the way God feels and thinks about you?

If you can answer "yes" to these questions, I'm delighted! You've probably received a revelation of the Father's love. I'm sure you're aware that there is always so much more of God's love for you to explore and enjoy, but you're in a rich and wonderful place; and once you're there, remember, you can always keep going deeper.

If you answered "no" to the questions above, you're not alone. In fact, many people struggle to take God's love personally. Perhaps it's easier for you to answer "yes" to the questions below.

• Do you find yourself wondering if God really loves you, and if so, why He does?
• Do you question whether or not God really wants the best for you?
• Do you believe God will love you more if you pray more, read the Bible more, give more tithes and offerings or serve others more?
• Do you try to perform because you think God will accept you if you do well enough?
• Do you think God loves other people more than He loves you?
• When you make a mistake, do you feel that God withholds His love or loves you less?

There was a time when I answered "yes" to all of these questions, but now I am becoming more and more secure in God's love for me. Getting to that point, though, was a process that included much time in the Word, prayer and a true heart's cry for a revelation of the love of the Father.

I believe your heart also cries out to know and experience God's love. I must tell you, though, that experiencing God's love for yourself may be a process for you, as it was for me. There are times when people have sudden life-changing revelations of God's love, but I have observed that the Lord usually leads people through a steady, deepening, ongoing process of coming to know His love in a personal way. That process may include anything from being healed from the wounds of the past to being set free from some form of oppression to forgiving someone or asking the Lord to forgive you of something that hinders your ability to receive His love. Your revelation of His love is never complete. He keeps revealing; you keep receiving—and you become more and more grounded in His awesome love for you as time goes on.

Many times, in the process of receiving God's love personally, lifelong thought patterns established by the enemy have to be broken. Replacing them with the truth of the Word is like having a glass of dirty water and pouring clean water into it. The more clean water you add, the more the dirty water spills out. Eventually, the glass is full of clean, clear water.

> The Lord usually leads people through a steady, deepening, ongoing process of coming to know His love in a personal way.

I remember when I was in prison and just beginning to discover that the Lord really loved me. One of the things I felt led to do was to speak aloud that God loved me. It was a simple exercise in which I spent four or five minutes speaking the words, "God loves me." In fact, I emphasized each word several times, saying, "*God* loves me. God *loves* me. God loves *me*." During the same time period, I was also praying the prayer in Ephesians 3:16–21, which you read in Leg 4 of this journey. I believe these two simple, practical ways of saturating yourself in God's love will help you gain more and more revelation of His love too.

Before we close this step, I want to make you aware of one sure hindrance to receiving the love of the Father—being angry with Him. People respond to God in anger for a variety of reasons, but the truth is that everything He does is rooted in His awesome love and, even when people don't understand the things that happen, no one has a right to be mad at God. If you are angry with Him, He still loves you, but it is extremely difficult for you to receive and experience the fullness of that love.

The journey into discovering, enjoying and being confident in God's love is ongoing. It's a wonderful process that brings joy and peace and wholeness in a way that nothing else can. I know, I really know, that God loves *you* so much. I know that He wants the best for you in every area of your life—and my prayer is that you will become more and more established in His love.

Moving Along

1. Go ahead, try it. Say, "*God* loves me. God *loves* me. God loves *me*." Keep saying that over and over, loud enough for your own ears to hear it. That will help begin to saturate your heart with the truth of His love for you.

2. List three ways the Lord has revealed or is revealing His love for you.

_____

_____

_____

3. Are you angry with God for any reason? If so, ask Him to forgive you and help you receive His love, using the prayer below or a similar one in your own words.

> *"Father, I have been angry with You because (<u>tell Him why you are angry</u>). I repent for my anger, and I ask You to forgive me. I pray that You would set me free and help me to receive Your love in greater and greater measure. In Jesus' name, Amen."*

4. Look up the scriptures listed below and write down what they say about God's love for you. Choose several to memorize and meditate on. Continue to meditate, even if it takes weeks or months, until these truths are established in your heart.

• Psalm 103:2-5 _____

_____

• Isaiah 54:10 _____

_____

• Jeremiah 31:3 _____

_____

• Lamentations 3:22, 23 _____

_____

• Zephaniah 3:17 _____

_____

• Romans 5:8 _____

Stepping Stones

For I am persuaded that neither death nor life,
nor angels nor principalities nor powers,
nor things present nor things to come, nor height nor depth,
nor any other created thing, shall be able to separate us
from the love of God which is in Christ Jesus our Lord.
Romans 8:38, 39

Behold what manner of love the Father has bestowed on us,
that we should be called children of God! . . .
1 John 3:1

Now hope does not disappoint,
because the love of God has been poured out
in our hearts by the Holy Spirit who was given to us.
Romans 5:5

Mile Markers

• God's greatest expression of love toward you took place when Jesus died on the cross.

• At the cross, Jesus took all the punishment you deserved and gave you all the life and goodness He deserved.

• God is God. Do not transfer the failures or perceived failures of your parent or caregiver (when they do not represent God's character and nature) onto Him.

• The truth about God's love is revealed through His Word and by His Spirit.

• God loves you. Take His love personally, and allow that revelation to take root in your heart.

• When it comes to knowing the Father's love, you never "arrive." There's always more!

Travel Journal

Here's your opportunity to take a break, kick back and be creative as you express what the Holy Spirit has taught you about the Father's awesome love for you.

P.S. Jesus loves you, this I know.

YOUR TRUE IDENTITY

Step 1: Know and Believe the Truth

Step 2: Accept Yourself

Step 3: Embrace God's Design

Dear Fellow Traveler,

I have often walked into a room or been sitting in a church service and heard the whispers: "She's the one who was in prison." That's true; it's a fact. I was in prison, but that fact does not shape or define my true identity. It was something that happened to me, but it is not who I am.

There was a time when my heart was like a catcher's mitt, and I "caught" every word or phrase by which anyone tried to identify me. As a child, when people remarked, "She's the pudgy one," I said, "Yep, that's me." As a high school student, if someone observed, "She's the mischievous one," I said, "Yep, that's me." Later, if people commented, "She's the pharmacist who drives a European sports car, drinks champagne and throws great parties," I said, "Yep, that's me."

Over the course of my life, all kinds of labels were tossed my way—and they all seemed to stick! They combined to make a false identity that did not begin to be dismantled until the Holy Spirit began to show me who I really was. I believe one of the reasons He took me through a season of focusing on what the Word says about my identity in Him, while I was in prison, was that He knew what I would face when I was released. He knew that, to this day, people would still say, "She's the one who was in prison." But because He has taught me who I really am, it does not bother me one bit!

Chances are, you too have had all sorts of labels thrown at you. People or situations may have attempted to define you, or you may have assumed certain things about yourself that have caused you to believe things about yourself that are not true. But the Lord knows who you are. He has given you an unshakable identity in Jesus. He created you and put within you treasures you may not have discovered yet. He wants you to be established in the identity *He* has given you in Christ, so that you can stand firm, be victorious and fulfill the great plans He has for your life.

As you journey through your life and grow in your relationship with the Lord, one of your sources of strength and stability will be a healthy, truth-based sense of personal identity—the God-given knowledge and understanding of who you are, what defines you, what distinguishes you from others, who you belong to and what He has put within you. Again, I am writing to you about your identity in Christ, which is the identity that never changes. It's solid and steady; it is the identity you can build your life upon, the identity that will keep you stable and strong, no matter what circumstances may hurl at you.

God bless you as you realize who you really are!
Mary

Step 1: Know and Believe the Truth

And you shall know the truth, and the truth shall make you free. John 8:32

The world would have you believe that you can identify and define yourself by the car you drive, the neighborhood you live in, the professional or educational levels you have attained or all sorts of other empty pursuits. (Trust me, I tried them all!) Besides that, the enemy will try to entice you to believe that your identity is determined by what you don't have. He will tell you, "You're the one with the oldest car in the parking lot," or "You're the one who wears the hand-me-downs," or "You're the one without a college degree," or "You're the one who's divorced" or "You're the one who was abandoned." The lies of the world and the lies of the enemy are equally potent. Either way, whether you're tempted to define yourself according to what you have or what you don't have, it's a trap. The first step toward developing a godly sense of identity is to know the truth, which you will only find in the Word of God.

Only as the Holy Spirit gives you revelation of the Word will you really find out who you are and begin to understand what's inside of you. Your primary source of identity must be spiritual, not natural. Your confidence must come from who the Lord *says* you are, not from who other people *think* you are. In other words, you are first and foremost a beloved, highly favored, called and chosen child of God. Secondarily, you are a schoolteacher, a physician, an airline attendant, a sales clerk, a mother or a father, a husband or a wife, a single person, a currently unemployed businessperson, an inmate or a person who fulfills all the other roles you must play in your life.

> Your primary source of identity must be spiritual, not natural. Your confidence must come from who the Lord *says* you are, not from who other people *think* you are.

I urge you to get your identity from the Word and not from the world. I remember when I had to make that choice, after years of trying to define myself by the trappings of life. The Holy Spirit showed me a vision in which I saw the palms of the Lord's hands. In the left hand, I saw all the "identity labels" I had tried to stitch onto myself or that others had tried to stick on me, labels such as: "reject," "loser," "convict," "thief," "felon," "greedy," "proud" and others. In the right hand, there were the names the Lord calls me: "beloved," "accepted," "anointed," "chosen," "called," "the apple of His eye," "one in whom He delights" and more. He then spoke to me, saying, "Mary, you choose. You choose who you are."

I challenge you as He challenged me. You choose. You can seek your identity in the successes of your life, or in your failures; you can look for it in the things that money can buy or in the things you can accomplish. But the only place you'll really find out who you are and be able to develop a solid, unshakable identity is in Jesus and in the truth of the Word. I really encourage you to take a trip through the Word of God with the intention of discovering your true identity. Ask the Holy Spirit to reveal to you who you really are as you read the Bible. To help you get started, I'd like to share with you just a few of the many statements that are true about you because you belong to Jesus.

- In Him, you are more than a conqueror (see Romans 8:37).
- In Him, you are beloved of God (see 1 Thessalonians 1:4).
- In Him, you are complete (see Colossians 2:10).
- In Him, you are always triumphant (see 2 Corinthians 2:14).
- In Him, you are free from condemnation (see Romans 8:1).
- In Him, you are called according to God's purpose (see Romans 8:28).
- In Him, you are a joint heir, sharing His inheritance (see Romans 8:17).
- In Him, you are a new creation (see 2 Corinthians 5:17).
- In Him, you are accepted (see Ephesians 1:6).
- In Him, you can do all things (see Philippians 4:13).

Moving Along

1. Listed below are some of the situations by which people often identify themselves. Check any that apply to you. Knowing where you have tried to get your identity will help you move past those things; realize that they are powerless to define you, and begin to get established in who the Lord has truly created you to be.

___ income

___ job or professional position

___ children

___ children's behavior

___ race

___ address or neighborhood

___ spouse's job or professional position

___ children's accomplishments

___ family name and / or history

___ education / degrees

___ car
___ investments
___ social life
___ trips or travel
___ skills, talents or abilities
___ divorce
___ abuse of any kind
___ alcoholism
___ legal trouble
___ failure in business
___ hobbies

___ friends / relationships
___ appearance (height, weight, being especially attractive, deformities)
___ church affiliation
___ bankruptcy
___ miscarriage or abortion
___ illness
___ drug substance
___ failure in school
___ sense of humor
___ being adopted

When you have completed this checklist, ask the Holy Spirit to help you stop seeking your primary identity in the areas you marked and to reveal your true identity, as it is found in the Word.

2. Read the following scriptures and write down what each one tells you about your identity in Jesus.

• John 1:12 _____

_____

• 2 Corinthians 5:21 _____

_____

• Ephesians 1:7, 8 _____

_____

• Ephesians 3:12 _____

_____

• Colossians 3:12 _____

_____

3. When you are reading the New Testament, you might want to mark or highlight every scripture that includes the words "in Him." Do the same with verses that include the words

"you are" or "we are," when pertaining to those who believe in Jesus, because that will help you clearly see who you are in Him. I suggest starting in Ephesians.

Stepping Stones

Your word is truth.
John 17:17

For we are His workmanship, created in
Christ Jesus for good works, which God prepared
beforehand that we should walk in them.
Ephesians 2:10

And you are complete in Him....
Colossians 2:10

And you shall know the truth,
and the truth shall make you free.
John 8:32

Step 2: Accept Yourself

For You formed my inward parts; You covered me in my mother's womb. I will praise You, for I am fearfully and wonderfully made; marvelous are Your works, and that my soul knows very well. Psalm 139:13, 14

The Lord has a tremendous blueprint for your life! Not only that, He has also designed you in such a way that you will be able to perfectly fulfill every wonderful thing He's ordained for you. His big-picture plan for your life is so detailed that He has handcrafted everything about you—your size and physical appearance, your gender, your race, your personality and even the moment of your birth. You are a delightful display of His creativity, a wonderful expression of His intricate thought and precise planning, a unique reflection of His heart and a lavish gift to the world in which you live. God's great desire is for you to fully accept and to totally embrace how He's made you and who He's created you to be.

On the other hand, the enemy never wants you to feel comfortable with yourself. He will whisper lies to you and even turn your emotions against you, in order to keep you from living in the truth of what God's Word says about you. He will use any means possible to convince you that you are not acceptable to yourself, to others or to the Lord. His primary weapon in this area is rejection, and he tries to infiltrate you with self-rejection and/or with the perception that others are rejecting you. Some of his tactics include:

You are a delightful display of His creativity, a wonderful expression of His intricate thought and precise planning, a unique reflection of His heart and a lavish gift to the world in which you live.

- feeling that you are a mistake
- feeling that you don't fit in
- feeling that there's something wrong with you
- feeling that you can't do anything right
- feeling guilty or condemned
- feeling that you need to please people
- feeling that you need to perform or be perfect
- feeling self-conscious
- feeling the need to defend yourself
- feeling self-pity
- feeling insecure

Notice that everything listed above is a feeling, and the enemy can use your feelings to penetrate your mind with lies. So, in order to overcome rejection and begin to accept yourself, you'll need to fight your feelings with the truth of the Word.

Psalm 139 is the Scripture passage the Lord used to help me climb out of the deep pit of rejection and begin to accept myself. I had struggled with a general sense of rejection all of my life, but never more than when I found myself in a prison cell, knowing that the next several years of my life were going to be spent behind bars. When I first read that Psalm, I thought, *Lord, You've got to be kidding. There's no way this can be talking about me!* But by that time, I knew that rejection was a tool of the enemy, and I knew that I had to wage war against him with the Word. I'd been entrenched in patterns of wrong thinking, self-rejection and perceived rejection for so long, that it took a while for me to truly accept myself. But I kept reading the words, "I am fearfully and wonderfully made," until I began to believe with all my heart that God really had created me according to a divine design, and that He—and I—were pleased with the way He'd made me.

I encourage you to do the same thing. Take a step toward accepting yourself by meditating on the truth that you are fearfully and wonderfully made and on other scriptures that reflect God's heart for you. The Lord is longing to demolish any strongholds of rejection or self-condemnation the enemy has built in your mind and to reveal to you the blueprint He has for your life. But remember, the plan is just for you. It won't work if you try to be someone else or if you don't accept yourself. His design for you works best when you are determined to be just the way He made you to be.

Moving Along

1. What do you like best about yourself?

_____

_____

2. Have you accepted yourself in the areas listed below? (Circle YES or NO)

- your gender .... YES / NO
- your race or nationality .... YES / NO
- your appearance (height, weight, features, hair color, eye color, etc.) .... YES / NO
- the time in which you were born .... YES / NO
- your parents .... YES / NO
- your siblings .... YES / NO
- your gifts and talents .... YES / NO
- your personality .... YES / NO

Look at the areas where you answered "no," and begin to thank the Lord out loud for each aspect of your life that He has designed, but that you have had difficulty accepting. Remember, He loves everything about you!

3. Look at Psalm 139:13, 14 and fill in the blanks.

Lord, You _____ my inward parts; you covered me in my mother's womb.

I will praise You, for I am _____ and _____ made.

_____ are Your works, and that my soul knows very well.

4. The Lord really wants you to see yourself the way He sees you. Take just a moment, get quiet, close your eyes and say, "Holy Spirit, show me how You see me" (or something similar). Write down what you sense from Him.

_____

_____

_____

Stepping Stones

Since you are precious in My sight,
since you are honored and I love you….
Isaiah 43:4 (NASB)

He chose us in Him before the foundation of the world,
that we should be holy and without blame before Him in love,
having predestined us to adoption as sons by Jesus Christ by
Himself, according to the good pleasure of His will,
to the praise of the glory of His grace,
by which He made us accepted in the Beloved.
Ephesians 1:4-6

For You formed my inward parts;
You covered me in my mother's womb.
I will praise You, for I am fearfully and wonderfully made;
marvelous are Your works, and that my soul knows very well.
Psalm 139:13, 14

Step 3: Embrace God's Design

But now, O Lord, You are our Father; we are the clay, and You our potter; and all we are the work of Your hand. Isaiah 64:8

Your identity in Jesus is solid and unchangeable, but in addition to that, you have a God-given personality through which you express your identity. For the longest time, I did not understand my personality. I did not know that my confidence, boldness, goal-orientation and ability to multitask were all part of my internal "wiring." Then I came across some information that described the four basic personality types: choleric, melancholy, sanguine and phlegmatic. Once I read about the strengths and weaknesses of each of these temperaments, I identified myself primarily as a choleric. Then I understood that part of the Lord's reason for designing me with such a strong personality was to help me fulfill His leadership call on my life. I also learned about the other personality types, which helped me understand and relate to people whose temperaments were quite different from mine.

> Once you know what general personality type you are, celebrate your strengths, pray through your weaknesses and be willing to make adjustments as the Holy Spirit leads.

I'll briefly describe each of the four personality types below in broad, general terms, but you can get more comprehensive information and personality tests in books related to this subject or on the internet.

Melancholy: Melancholies are the creative and thoughtful types. They are loyal, sensitive and self-sacrificing. Their strengths include being conscientious, detail-oriented, concerned about others, content to stay out of the limelight and thorough. Their weaknesses include low self-esteem, remembering the bad instead of the good, having standards that are too high, being skeptical or suspicious of others and people-pleasing.

Sanguine: Sanguines love to laugh and have fun! They love people, make friends easily and have a good sense of humor. Their strengths include enthusiasm, the ability to apologize and forgive quickly, cheerfulness, the ability to live in the moment, and the desire to gather and entertain groups of people. Their weaknesses include not letting others speak, a tendency to exaggerate, restlessness, self-centeredness and forgetting obligations or not carrying out responsibilities.

Phlegmatic: Phlegmatics think everything is all right, all the time. They are relaxed and pleasant, and they tend to be good administrators. Their strengths include steadiness, balance, the ability to handle pressure well, patience and the ability to mediate conflict. Their weaknesses include a lack of enthusiasm, a tendency to compromise too much, resistance to change, indecisiveness and self-righteousness.

Choleric: Cholerics are born leaders. They are strong, confident and independent. Their strengths include decisiveness, a strong work ethic, willingness to confront and correct wrongs, the ability to produce results and the ability to multitask. Their weaknesses include bossiness, insensitivity, failing to affirm others, not looking closely enough at details and the inability to relax.

You can have aspects of all four basic personality types, but chances are that your predominant personality type will fall into one of the four categories above. Looking at temperaments is not for the purpose of putting labels on people, but to help you identify the strengths and weaknesses associated with your basic wiring. Once you know what general personality type you are, celebrate your strengths, pray through your weaknesses and be willing to make adjustments as the Holy Spirit leads. Ask Him to help you know how to work with your personality and use it to accomplish His purposes for your life. Ultimately, understanding your personality type will help you accept yourself and allow your identity to be expressed in a way that maximizes everything God has put inside of you.

Moving Along

1. What do you think your predominant personality type is?

_____

2. List three strengths of your personality. Thank the Lord for them. Then list three weaknesses of your personality and ask the Holy Spirit to help you with them.

_____

_____

_____

_____

_____

3. How do you think your personality type may relate to God's purposes for your life?

_____

_____

Stepping Stones

He fashions their hearts individually;
He considers all their works.
Psalm 33:15

For as we have many members in one body,
but all the members do not have the same function….
Romans 12:4

But now God has set the members, each one of them,
in the body just as He pleased.
1 Corinthians 12:18

But now, O Lord, You are our Father;
we are the clay, and You our potter;
and all we are the work of Your hand.
Isaiah 64:8

Mile Markers

• Your true identity is found in the Word of God, not in anything the world offers.

• Define yourself according to the truth of God's Word. Know the truth and believe it for yourself.

• Accept yourself the way God made you. Thank Him for doing such a great job with you!

• Do not let the enemy cause you to feel rejected. Resist rejection by focusing on God's love for you and keeping a thankful heart.

• There are four basic personality types: melancholy, sanguine, phlegmatic and choleric.

• Understand your personality, and discover how it is part of the way the Lord has wired you in order for you to accomplish His purposes for your life. Celebrate your strengths, and pray through your weaknesses.

Travel Journal

Here's your opportunity to take a break, kick back and be creative as you express what the Holy Spirit has taught you about who you really are.

P.S. Remember, you're one of a kind!

GOD'S PURPOSE FOR YOUR LIFE

Step 1: Discover Your Destiny

Step 2: Know Your Season

Step 3: Align Your Life with God's Purpose

Dear Fellow Traveler,

One of the most exciting and fulfilling aspects of your journey through life is to be able to do what God has called and created you to do. There is something deep inside of you that yearns to discover and fulfill His purpose for your life, a hidden passion in your heart that God wants you to get in touch with; it's something that will remain restless until you do—and it's never too late to begin. As I shared with you in Leg Six of our journey, the Lord has fashioned you in such a way that you will find your greatest joy, your most exhilarating challenge, your deepest sense of peace and accomplishment only as you understand why He made you and what He wants you do with your days upon the earth.

Prison is not a very likely place for a person to be encouraged about her future, much less to discover a God-given destiny. But that's where it happened for me. One day, I read Jeremiah 29:11, which reads, "'For I know the plans I have for you' declares the Lord, 'plans to prosper you and not to harm you, plans to give you hope and a future'" (NIV). In response to those words, I said in my heart, "No way, Lord. You have got to be kidding. You're telling me that You have good plans for *me?* You want me to believe that You have a future and a hope for *me?* But look where I am!"

But that scripture seemed to follow me everywhere I went. Someone would send me a greeting card with Jeremiah 29:11 on it, or I would read it in a book I borrowed from the chapel library or a minister on television would quote it. I couldn't get away from it, so I finally decided to believe it! Once I opened my heart to the possibility that the Lord was asking me to believe Him for a good future and to take hold of the hope He offered me, the Holy Spirit began to speak promises to me and give me vision for my life—vision far beyond my current circumstances. At times, contending for my destiny has been a fierce battle, but it has always been worth it. I am now living some of the promises the Lord gave me while I was in prison.

You may be in a prison of your own. It may not be surrounded with razor wire; it may not have visible bars; you may not be physically handcuffed or shackled. But you may be locked in a cell of fear, disappointment, anxiety, loneliness, pride, anger, guilt, lack, rejection or any number of other challenges. Regardless of your circumstances, the Holy Spirit wants to speak destiny to you. Wherever you are, even if you are facing obstacles, He wants to give you greater understanding and ability to walk in the purpose for which He created you. And I'll let you in on a secret: many times, when you begin to hear and respond to His whispers of destiny, your chains begin to fall off.

I am filled with hope when I think about the great future God has in store for you. Be encouraged as you walk out His call upon your life!

God bless you as you discover His destiny for you!
Mary

Step 1: Discover Your Destiny

"Eye has not seen, nor ear heard, nor have entered into the heart of man the things which God has prepared for those who love Him." But God has revealed them to us through His Spirit.... 1 Corinthians 2:9, 10

The discovery of your destiny—God's purpose and intention for your life—starts with believing that He has a unique plan that only you can fulfill, and you are especially designed to fulfill it. This is the place where your passions, giftings, talents, training, experiences, personality and the influences that have shaped you all come together. It's like a tailor-made suit that fits only you, fits you to perfection and wouldn't even look good on anybody else!

One of the reasons the Lord so eagerly wants you to discover His purpose for your life is that walking in your destiny births intimacy with Him in a way that nothing else can. Amos 3:3 says, "Can two walk together, unless they are agreed?" When you know God's plans for your life, you can agree with Him, and the two of you can walk together with shared vision, united in purpose.

When I write that the Holy Spirit is longing to reveal destiny to you, I am not talking about a mystical experience, but about the practical ways He helps you discover what you were meant to do. You'll find clues to your destiny as you think about what you enjoy, your areas of proficiency and what you believe is worth fighting for. It's possible that your hobbies and interests could be some of the ingredients of your destiny. You see, the Lord begins to equip you for destiny long before you recognize what that destiny is, and He inclines you toward the things that are part of that purpose. I believe He's been preparing you for a long time, and you may already be advancing in His plans without even knowing it.

> One of the reasons the Lord so eagerly wants you to discover His purpose for your life is that walking in your destiny births intimacy with Him in a way that nothing else can.

I once heard someone offer a concise piece of advice concerning how to discover your destiny: "Look at what's in your heart and what's in your hand." In other words, what do you long for, what is the desire of your heart, what are you already doing, what do you have access to, and what do you have the ability to do? I really encourage you to prayerfully consider what you have in your heart and what you have in your hand. And as you do, don't be surprised if destiny begins to unfold.

As much as the Holy Spirit wants you to know and understand your purpose, the enemy also wants to render you ineffective and prevent you from achieving and enjoying all that God has for you. He will attempt to:

- Distract you and divert your focus from God's destiny for your life.
- Discourage you.
- Keep you busy doing things that are good, but not necessarily part of your destiny assignment.
- Dull your passion by stealing your time or desire to pursue it.
- Lead you into the trap of comparing yourself with others.
- Infect you with fear of failure.
- Puff you up with pride.
- Tell you that your dream is stupid.
- Devalue your gifts, abilities or desires.
- Cause you to be unwilling to move in the direction of your dream until you understand it completely.
- Tell you that you are not worthy.
- Tell you that God has a big plan for "the world," but not a specific, individualized plan for you.
- Get you to procrastinate.
- Push you to move too quickly.

When the enemy uses these tactics against you, resist him. Fight back with the truth of the Word and by thanking the Lord for the good plans He has for you.

God has an assignment for you to complete, a victory for you to apprehend, an aspect of glory for you to give to Him. He has a destiny for you to fulfill, but it, in turn, will fulfill you. Keep walking toward it, and if you've already discovered it, keep marching on.

Moving Along

1. What gifts or abilities do you have that you believe God has given you in order to fulfill His purpose for your life?

_____

_____

2. Are you currently investing time, money or energy in anything you don't really believe is part of your destiny? If so, what adjustments do you need to make in order to be better aligned with God's plans for your life?

_____

_____

_____

3. What's in your heart and what's in your hand?

_____

_____

4. Pray and ask the Holy Spirit to reveal destiny to you. Use the prayer below or pray a similar one in your own words.

> *Father, I want to know the plans You have for my life. Lord, begin to show me how to use the resources I have right now, the talents you've given to me, even if I can't recognize them. Lord, begin to help me move forward into the destiny You have for me. Thank You for having such great plans for me! In Jesus' name, Amen.*

Stepping Stones

Trust in the Lord, and do good; dwell in the land,
and feed on His faithfulness.
Delight yourself also in the Lord,
and He shall give you the desires of your heart.
Commit your way to the Lord, trust also in Him,
and He shall bring it to pass.
Psalm 37:3-5

"For I know the plans I have for you," declares the Lord,
"plans to prosper you and not to harm you,
plans to give you hope and a future."
Jeremiah 29:11(NIV)

He reveals deep and secret things; He knows what is in the darkness,
and light dwells with Him.
Daniel 2:22

"Eye has not seen, nor ear heard,
nor have entered into the heart of man
the things which God has prepared for those who love Him."
But God has revealed them to us through His Spirit. . . .
1 Corinthians 2:9, 10

Step 2: Know Your Season

To everything there is a season, a time for every purpose under heaven.
Ecclesiastes 3:1

Perceiving your destiny is like seeing a computer-generated image of a house you plan to build. The picture will help you know where you will live once the home is finished and you have settled in. The image will encourage you because you know it will be a reality someday; but until the lot is prepared, the foundation is laid, the frame is erected and the building is complete, it will not be ready for you to move into.

As you discover God's purpose for your life, the Holy Spirit will reveal aspects of destiny to you and may give you a general understanding of His big-pic-

> You are in the process of fulfilling your destiny, and you will always be in the process of fulfilling it because you never "retire" from God's purpose.

ture plans for you. But being able to perceive your destiny does not mean that its ultimate fulfillment is necessarily near. You are in the process of fulfilling it, and you will always be in the process of fulfilling it because you never "retire" from God's purpose. He will be using you and allowing you to fulfill His call until you breathe your last breath. But as you journey through your life, there will be moments when you receive a specific revelation or strategy or when you have an opportunity to respond to something that will take you miles down the road of your destiny. You simply have to know the times and seasons of God's plans and to know what to do when.

For example, if the Lord shows you that you are going to be president of the United States, that does not mean you should register as a candidate in the next election and begin to buy furniture that would look nice in the residence at the White House. If the Lord shows you that you will own your own business someday, that does not mean you should immediately quit the job you have now.

Several years ago, I was certain the Lord was preparing me to move into a new apartment. I packed my belongings, labeled the boxes and stacked them so that they could be easily loaded onto the moving truck. Six months later, they were still stacked. A year later, they were *still* stacked! Fourteen months later, the Lord did move me into a new place. I had accurately perceived the change He wanted to bring to my life, but I was extremely premature in my preparations! You may be like I am, having a tendency to move too quickly, or you may be inclined to lag behind. Either way, it's important that we all understand God's timing and keep rank and pace with it.

> Living in obedience to the Word and in communion with the Holy Spirit will help you recognize the season changes in your life.

The Lord will take you through a variety of seasons as you walk the path of your purpose. The more you understand times and seasons, the more you can cooperate with what the Holy Spirit is doing in your life. When you do not understand the season you are in, you may resist the work of the Holy Spirit or the tools He sends to help you—simply because you are not aware of what He is doing or how He is working. I really encourage you to ask Him what season you are in right now and to be open to season changes as the Lord directs.

I have never known anyone who did not walk through seasons of preparation as he or she made progress in the process of fulfilling God's purpose. In the midst of preparation, you may go through seasons of challenge, seasons of equipping (spiritual and/or natural), seasons when God seems silent (during those times, just keep doing the last thing He told you to do, and walk in the fruit of the Spirit, which I'll write about in Leg 11), seasons when you feel you are in the wilderness, season and deliverance, seasons of spiritual growth and seasons of increased revelation and fresh strategy.

Living in obedience to the Word and in communion with the Holy Spirit will help you recognize the season changes in your life. He will reveal to you that a change is coming, and you will sense His "indicators" telling you it's time for a turn. You will notice that His grace for certain tasks, situations or commitments has lifted. Desires will begin to stir inside of you in a brand-new way, fresh opportunities will begin to present themselves and strategies will be revealed. In the midst of God-ordained transitions, you must not consult your emotions. When it is time for a change, you may feel frustrated, fearful, anxious or confused, but those are nothing more than feelings—and feelings are fickle. Stay tethered to the Word, spend much time in prayer, listen to wise counsel and seek the Lord with all your heart. After all, He's ordering every single one of your steps.

Just as each natural season has its own unique beauty, so does every season in the Lord. I encourage you to enjoy each one, and when it's time for a change, walk wisely with the Holy Spirit!

Moving Along

1. Can you identify specific seasons the Lord has brought you through? What were they? What indicated season changes for you?

_____

_____

_____

2. Can you remember a time when the grace lifted for a certain situation in your life and a change followed soon afterward? Does that give you insight into one of the ways of God?

_____

_____

3. Can you identify any ways the Holy Spirit may be trying to help you know what season you are in right now? For instance, is there a Scripture verse you see everywhere you look? Is there a line from a song that keeps replaying itself in your head? Do you keep seeing the same words or phrases? Do you find yourself repeatedly praying about an issue, but it feels "fresh" every time?

_____

_____

_____

4. How would you define the season you are in right now? If you are not sure, pray the prayer below, or a similar one in your own words.

_____

_____

Father, I am asking for understanding and revelation of what season I am in. Lord, I want to live my life according to Your timing for me. Lord, show me if I am moving too fast or too slow in any area of my life. Help me to always walk in rank and in pace with You. In Jesus' name, Amen.

Stepping Stones

The steps of a good man are ordered by the Lord,
and He delights in His way.
Psalm 37:23

And He changes the times and the seasons;
He removes kings and raises up kings;
He gives wisdom to the wise
and knowledge to those who have understanding.
Daniel 2:21

And let us not grow weary while doing good,
for in due season we shall reap
if we do not lose heart.
Galatians 6:9

To everything there is a season,
a time for every purpose under heaven.
Ecclesiastes 3:1

Step 3: Align Your Life with God's Purpose

That you may be filled with the knowledge of His will in all wisdom and spiritual understanding; that you may walk worthy of the Lord, fully pleasing Him, being fruitful in every good work and increasing in the knowledge of God.
Colossians 1:9, 10

When I write to you of aligning your life with God's purpose, what I mean is that you are not only to be sensitive to God's timing, but that in each season, you are to be obedient to do what He asks you to do. For instance, as He moves you along in your destiny, there may be a time in which He wants to heal the broken places in your heart so you will be stronger and more whole in the days to come. In order to cooperate with Him, you may have to align your life with that purpose by reading books on inner healing, seeking prayer from people who can help, meditating on scriptures that are unfamiliar or praying about situations you haven't prayed about before. But part of the way you align yourself with His purpose is to find out where His finger is on your life and to let His focus be your focus. In other words, if He is trying to help you deal with pride, don't try to get Him to help you be a better steward of your resources. When He moves to focus on your finances, then you can ask Him to help you with your stewardship.

> Part of the way you align yourself with His purpose is to find out where His finger is on your life and to let His focus be your focus.

I remember when I was transferred to a halfway house as part of a prison work-release program and assigned to a job at the V.A. Hospital in Dallas. Technology had exploded so rapidly during my incarceration that I did not even know how to create a word-processing document. My job at the V.A. required me to learn basic computer skills, which laid the foundation for the computer skills I have needed on every job since that time and that I now need in order to run a ministry.

The Holy Spirit was focused on enabling me to develop the skills I would need in the future, even though I had not needed them in my career before prison. Instead of thinking, *Well, I never needed to know how to operate this software before…,* I took advantage of the opportunity to learn. Little did I know at that time that I would not return to practicing pharmacy again. The Lord had a different future in store for me—one that required some computer proficiency!

When you desire to align your life with God's purposes, it is not only important that you stay focused and avail yourself of the opportunities He gives you, it is also critical that you let go of the past. You simply cannot move into your future if the cords of your past are keeping you bound.

The Bible says that "faith without works is dead" (James 2:26), so seek the Lord to know when to step out and exercise your faith in a tangible, practical way. When it is time to respond to what God has put in your heart, take some sort of action. For example, if the Lord has spoken to you that now is the time to pursue becoming a CPA, investigate the courses you need to take. Find out how much they will cost, and begin saving the money for them. Look down the road toward the CPA exam, and do everything you can do now in order to be prepared for it.

Maybe you have been feeling the nudges of the Holy Spirit in the area of health or nutrition. You may wonder why I would mention this when we speak of destiny—because your body is the temple of the Holy Spirit (see 1 Corinthians 6:19), and the Lord knows the level of health and strength you will need in order to fulfill His purposes. If the Holy Spirit leads you to eliminate sugar from your diet, start exercising, get more sleep or take vitamins, trust His leading and obey.

Aligning your life with God's plan is an individual pursuit. It's wonderful when He gives you a "buddy in the battle," but you must always hear Him for yourself on a deeply personal level.

Aligning your life with God's plan is an individual pursuit. It's wonderful when He gives you a "buddy in the battle," but you must always hear Him for yourself on a deeply personal level while you also make sure you are living in obedience to His Word. You can't look at the liberty or restrictions the Lord gives to someone else; you have to know what He's requiring of you. For example, your friend may be able to go to the movie and have popcorn, a candy bar and a soft drink. You, on the other hand, may know that you can only have bottled water because the Lord is helping you learn to eat and drink more healthily. After the movie, you may go shopping with that same friend, and you may be able to make purchases that she can't because the Lord is dealing with her in the area of spending money. When you're serious about aligning your life with God's purpose, you have to be focused on what He's asking *you* to do and be diligent to obey.

You may think that food choices or spending habits don't seem very important in the grand scheme of your destiny, but I remind you that "Whoever can be trusted with very little can also be trusted with much" (Luke 16:10, NIV), and that the "little foxes" spoil the vine (see Song of Songs 2:15). God is for you; the Holy Spirit will help you. You do your part, and He will be faithful to bring to pass all that He has spoken to you!

Moving Along

1. Is the Holy Spirit telling you to do something that could be connected to your destiny? What is it? How can you wisely exercise your faith in what He has spoken to you?

_____

_____

2. What is God requiring of you that He may not be requiring of the people around you? Write your answer below—and know that it's good for you!

_____

_____

3. Have you aligned your life with God's purposes, as best you know how, in the following areas? (Circle YES or NO)

- health and nutrition .... YES / NO
- spending habits .... YES / NO
- investments .... YES / NO
- giving (whether giving money, time, old clothes or furniture, etc.)............ YES / NO
- exercise .... YES / NO
- integrity .... YES / NO
- spiritual life .... YES / NO
- job or career .... YES / NO
- family .... YES / NO
- marriage .... YES / NO
- time management .... YES / NO
- entertainment .... YES / NO

For the items on which you circled no, repent and ask the Holy Spirit to help you follow His leading in that area.

4. There may be some little things God wants to be able to trust you with now, so that He can begin to trust you with greater things in the days to come. Can you identify any of those things? What are they?

_____

_____

_____

Stepping Stones

Whoever can be trusted with very little
can also be trusted with much….
Luke 16:10 (NIV)

And we know that all things work together for good
to those who love God,
to those who are called according to His purpose.
Romans 8:28

He who calls you is faithful, who also will do it.
1 Thessalonians 5:24

Tthat you may be filled with the knowledge of His will
in all wisdom and spiritual understanding;
that you may walk worthy of the Lord, fully pleasing Him,
being fruitful in every good work and
increasing in the knowledge of God.
Colossians 1:9, 10

Mile Markers

• God has a great purpose for your life, and it's divinely designed for you. Discovering your destiny breeds intimacy with the Lord.

• Your abilities and interests may be connected to God's destiny for your life.

• The enemy does not want you to discover God's purpose for your life. Recognize his tactics, and resist him with the truth of the Word and with thanksgiving.

• Understanding the times and seasons of your life will help you cooperate with the Holy Spirit.

• When seasons change, do not let your emotions lead you. Instead, pay attention to spiritual indicators, such as the lifting of grace, God-given opportunities, God-given desires and divine revelation and strategies.

• Align your life with God's purpose by being obedient to do what He asks you to do in every season. Know what the Holy Spirit is focused on in your life, and stay focused on that until He leads you to move on.

• Remember to be faithful in the little things.

Travel Journal

Here's your opportunity to take a break, kick back and be creative as you express what the Holy Spirit has taught you about God's great purposes for your life.

P.S. He's preparing you now for great things later!

HEART ATTITUDES

Step 1: Be Good Ground

Step 2: Live from the Inside Out

Step 3: Cultivate an Excellent Spirit

Dear Fellow Traveler,

On this Leg of the journey, I'd like to share with you a major revelation I received while in prison—a revelation that revolutionized the way I thought, spoke and acted. Let me start by telling you that when I arrived at the federal prison in Benton, Texas, I had nothing but a suitcase and a great big, multifaceted bad attitude! I was proud, selfish, impatient, ungracious, independent, rebellious and judgmental. In my pre-prison life, I had been so driven to perform that I had never given much thought to my motives or to my attitudes; I was only interested in results. I knew that it was possible to "do" right or to "do" wrong, but I did not know to consider the underlying reasons and intentions behind my actions.

After the Holy Spirit touched my life and I had started reading the Word and learning to pray, I was shocked when He began to deal with the attitudes in my heart. He led me to address the unforgiveness I harbored toward the judge and the twelve jurors who had convicted me and sent me to prison. He was teaching me a vital principle for my spiritual life: God works from the inside out.

Perhaps I was expecting the Lord to make me "religious"—to improve my behavior, clean up my language and start attending chapel services. But there was nothing religious about the way He pursued me. He was simply trying to get my heart in tune with His, which is what develops true relationship with Him. He zeroed in on my heart attitudes because He knew that once He had my heart, my behavior would change and begin to reflect the transformation He was working within me. With a holy aggression, He set about getting my heart in a condition in which I could begin to know Him, commune with Him, grasp His purpose for my life and obey Him.

I know the Holy Spirit is pursuing you too, and I suspect He's working from the inside out. Perhaps He has His finger on a rebellious attitude toward your boss or on anger toward God. Maybe He is trying to set you free from judging other people and thinking you are better than they are or from dishonoring your parents. There are any number of attitudes He may be wanting to deal with, so I encourage you to cooperate with Him. He really longs to capture your heart. Even if you gave it to Him many years ago, I believe He wants to apprehend it afresh and take you into a new dimension of communion with Him. Even if you are intimate with the Lord already, I believe He wants to take you deeper.

Part of the journey into spiritual maturity is to allow the Holy Spirit to deal with your attitudes—and to realize that everything He touches *can* be changed.

God bless you as He captures your heart!
Mary

Step 1: Be Good Ground

But other seed fell on good ground and yielded a crop that sprang up, increased and produced: some thirtyfold, some sixty, and some a hundred. Mark 4:8

How's your heart? I remember when I could not even begin to answer that question because I was completely out of touch with what was going on inside of me. That really began to change one day when I read the following story in Mark 4.

> *And it happened, as he sowed, that some seed fell by the wayside; and the birds of the air came and devoured it. Some fell on stony ground, where it did not have much earth; and immediately it sprang up because it had no depth of earth. But when the sun was up it was scorched, and because it had not root it withered away. And some seed fell among thorns; and the thorns grew up and choked it, and it yielded no crop. But other seed fell on good ground and yielded a crop that sprang up, increased and produced: some thirtyfold, some sixty, and some a hundred.*
>
> *Mark 4:4-8*

I then read Jesus' interpretation of this parable and realized that the seed represents the Word of God, and each type of ground represents a particular attitude or condition of heart. The Holy Spirit revealed to me that the "ground" in my heart determined how deeply the Word would take root in me and how effective it would be in my life. As you consider what kind of ground is in your heart, I'll offer a brief explanation of the four conditions of heart about which Jesus spoke in Mark 4.

1. *The wayside heart.* A heart by the wayside is one from which the enemy can quickly steal the Word. If you have this kind of heart, you hear the Word, but cannot stand on it or apply it to your life. The wayside is unplowed ground, which says to me that this kind of heart is unbroken and proud. It may be a heart that resists the softening or "tilling" of the Holy Spirit and is therefore hardened. For in-

"But other seed fell on good ground and yielded a crop that sprang up, increased and produced: some thirtyfold, some sixty, and some a hundred."

stance, when He leads you to forgive someone and you refuse, your heart gets harder. When you listen to His voice and obey, your heart gets softer. In order for a wayside heart to become good soil, it is necessary to allow the Holy Spirit to break up the ground by being diligent to take the Word personally, guarding your heart and submitting to His direction. That way, you will allow the Word to sink in so the enemy cannot pluck it up.

2. *The stony heart.* A stony heart receives the Word with excitement, but loses it the moment enthusiasm is challenged. A stony heart is not hardened to the Word, but is too shallow to hold onto it. It is easily offended, and in the face of obstacles it will trade the truth of the Word for the fickleness of emotions. For instance, I know a woman who said she believed Jeremiah 29:11. She was so thrilled that the Lord had plans for good and not evil for her life and that He wanted to give her a hope and a future. But the minute something didn't go her way, she decided that verse wasn't really true, and that God was trying to trick her. In order to remove the stones from a heart, a person must make a conscious decision to believe the Word, no matter what, and refuse to let emotions or circumstances change what he or she believes.

3. *The thorny heart.* A heart full of thorns is distracted and unfocused. It is tilled enough and deep enough to nurture the Word, but its soil is not pure. Within the soil is a mixture of things that will grow up to choke the fruit of the Word in a person's life. For example, a person with a thorny heart may know and believe the Word, but may also be easily distracted and allow the cares of this world to consume time and energy. A thorny heart is also susceptible to lusts and desires that are contrary to God's will and can be deceived into believing that money or possessions will bring fulfillment. In order to get the thorns out, a person needs to seek the things of God above all else, be diligent to stay focused on the Word and to pursue a growing, vibrant relationship with the Lord. When the heart is focused and priorities are in order, the Word is effective.

4. *The "good ground" heart.* Good ground is the product of careful tending as people aggressively follow the Holy Spirit as He leads them to guard their hearts, stay humble and tender, be stable and focused, deal with impurities and "catch the little foxes" that "spoil the vine." In good ground, the seed of the Word settles into deep, rich soil and is jealously guarded so that it cannot be stolen; it is received with joy and then nurtured with steadfast confidence and prayer; it much bears fruit.

Getting to the point of having good ground in your heart is important, but keeping it good is equally critical. You maintain it the same way you obtain it—by obeying the Word and following the Holy Spirit. The cultivation of good ground in your life is the way the Holy Spirit begins to work from the inside out!

Moving Along

1. Read Proverbs 4:23. How can you personally apply this verse in your life?

_____

_____

_____

2. Is there any untilled soil in your heart—someone you need to forgive, an action the Holy Spirit is asking you to take, something you need to give away, something you need to stop doing or something He wants you to start doing? What is it, and how should you respond?

_____

_____

3. Are there any thorny places in your heart, any areas in which the Word is being choked by worry, busyness or ungodly desires? What are the "thorns" that distract you from pursuing the things of God?

_____

_____

4. Have you ever seen the fruit of good ground in your heart? If so, what was it? If not, what changes do you need to make in order to begin to improve the condition of your soil?

_____

_____

_____

Stepping Stones

Keep your heart with all diligence,
for out of it spring the issues of life.
Proverbs 4:23

Thorns and snares are in the way of the perverse;
he who guards his soul will be far from them.
Proverbs 22:5

Sow for yourselves righteousness; reap in mercy;
break up your fallow ground, for it is time to seek the Lord,
till He comes and rains righteousness on you.
Hosea 10:12

"But other seed fell on good ground and yielded a crop
that sprang up, increased and produced:
some thirtyfold, some sixty, and some a hundred."
Mark 4:8

Step 2: Live from the Inside Out

Now may the God of peace Himself sanctify you completely; and may your whole spirit, soul, and body be preserved blameless at the coming of our Lord Jesus Christ. 1 Thessalonians 5:23

When I write to you of "living from the inside out," I am referring to the process of allowing the truth of the Word and the ministry of the Holy Spirit to direct what you think, say and do. It means being sensitive internally and being keenly aware of your attitudes, thoughts, motives and intentions. It's not just doing the right thing, but doing the right thing in the right spirit.

The foundation of living from the inside out comes from understanding that God created you as a three-part being. Your *spirit* is the deepest part of you, who you really are, the part of you that communes with the Holy Spirit. Your *soul* is comprised of your mind, your will and your emotions. Your *body* is your physical being, the part that houses your soul and your spirit. So, you *are* a spirit; you *have* a soul; and you *live in* a body.

After you are born again, you have the ability to live from your spirit instead of from your soul or your body. When you live from your soul, you make decisions and take actions based on what you think, want or feel. When you live from your body, you allow your thoughts and behavior to be determined or affected by what you see, hear, touch, taste or smell. Living from the inside out is the process of learning to recognize the leading of the Holy Spirit, who speaks in your spirit, and defer to that instead of allowing your soul or your body to be in control.

The Holy Spirit communes with your spirit, but you process His voice through your soul and express it through your body, often with the words of your mouth, your body language or your actions. This is why the enemy wants to wound your soul (inflict emotional pain) and twist your thinking. If he can do that, you can easily misinterpret what the Holy Spirit is speaking to you because it passes through the filter of wrong thinking, hurt feelings or an unwillingness to obey. When this happens, your thoughts, actions and words will be tainted with the wounds he has inflicted, such as fear, rejection, selfishness, anger or doubt.

The wounds of the soul lead to bad heart attitudes. They can cause you to be selfish, to act out of a desire for revenge because you are offended or to make an unwise decision out of anger or hurt. So, in order for your heart attitudes to line up with the Word, the soul needs to be cleansed through repentance and healed by the power of the Holy Spirit. And when the soul is clean and whole, the heart attitudes will be right, and the fruit will be good.

Healing is the work of the Holy Spirit, and He is longing to restore your soul. If you need Him to bring wholeness to your soul, pray the prayer below or a similar one in your own words.

> *Holy Spirit, I ask You to reveal to me any areas in my heart that the enemy has wounded, and to touch them with Your healing power. I repent for every bad attitude (list specific bad attitudes He shows you) that has resulted from wounds in my heart, and I ask You to help me correct them. In Jesus' name, Amen.*

Moving Along

1. In your own words, what does it mean to "live from the inside out?" How does this phrase practically apply to your life?

_____

_____

2. Say aloud, "I am a spirit; I have a soul; and I live in a body." Now, ask the Holy Spirit to help you live from your spirit and not from your soul or your body.

3. Can you remember any times when you let your body (your five senses) determine a specific course of action? What were they? (For example, have you ever smelled a freshly baked cake and then eaten so much of it that you ended up sick?) How might you respond differently now?

_____

_____

_____

4. Have you ever been healed from a wound in your soul (an emotional hurt)? What difference did that healing make in your attitudes and actions?

_____

_____

_____

Stepping Stones

He restores my soul. . . .
Psalm 23:3

Create in me a clean heart, O God,
and renew a steadfast spirit within me.
Psalm 51:10

A good man out of the good treasure of his heart brings forth good things,
and an evil man out of the evil treasure brings forth evil things.
Matthew 12:35

Since you have purified your souls in obeying the truth through
the Spirit in sincere love of the brethren,
love one another fervently with a pure heart,
having been born again, not of corruptible seed but incorruptible,
through the Word of God which lives and abides forever…
1 Peter 1:22, 23

Now may the God of peace Himself sanctify you completely;
and may your whole spirit, soul, and body be preserved blameless
at the coming of our Lord Jesus Christ.
1 Thessalonians 5:23

Step 3: Cultivate an Excellent Spirit

I will give you a new heart and put a new spirit within you…. Ezekiel 36:26

In Christian circles, you may hear the word *spirit* used several different ways. It is used in reference to the Holy Spirit, to evil spirits, to a person's spirit and to describe the heart attitude in which something is said or done. When I write to you about an excellent spirit, I am referring to the attitudes or motives behind everything you do. To have an excellent spirit to do the right thing, with the right attitude, from the right motive— even when no one is looking. An excellent spirit has nothing to do with pleasing people; it has everything to do with honoring the Lord and reflecting His excellent nature.

Having an excellent spirit means that you allow the Holy Spirit to reveal to you His standards and His strategy for whatever you are doing, and you do it as though you are working for Him.

I remember one of the first times the Holy Spirit challenged me to have an excellent spirit. One of my duties in prison was to clean the windows in the television room. One day, I worked hard and thought I had done a good job, even though I had hurried through the task so I could go back to my cell. As I rushed away, the Holy Spirit spoke to my heart and said, "Mary, you missed a section."

A quick glance at the windows revealed that I had indeed skipped one pane, which was still smudged and spotted. My first thought was that, within minutes, inmates would put their hands all over it and mess it up again. But the Holy Spirit reminded me that I had recently heard a sermon about having an excellent spirit, which, as I've already written, includes doing the right thing even when no one is watching. I knew that, in order to respond with an excellent spirit, I had to take my bottle of window cleaner and my paper towels back to that one pane and clean it until it matched the others. When I finished, a sense of strength welled up inside of me, not because the window sparkled, but because I was learning how to practically exercise an excellent spirit.

Now, there is a difference between excellence and perfection. Perfectionism is not an admirable quality (in fact, it is a type of bondage), but excellence is. Having an excellent spirit does not mean that you aim for a flawless performance, but that you allow the Holy Spirit to reveal to you His standards and His strategy for whatever you are doing, and you do it as though you are working for Him. Some of the characteristics of an excellent spirit are:

- Integrity
- Honesty
- Persistence
- Humility
- Consistency
- Valuing the tasks or assignments given to you
- Focusing on quality
- Desiring for things to be as well done or well said as possible
- Going beyond the call of duty
- Having a servant's heart
- Keeping your word
- Doing all things as unto the Lord

The enemy does not want you to be excellent, and he will attempt to keep you in mediocrity using some of the following:

- Comparison
- Failure to release the past and embrace the future
- Self-pity or a victim mentality
- Fear
- Pride
- Hard-heartedness
- Laziness
- Complacency
- Rebellion
- Offense
- Familiarity
- Compromise

I encourage you to resist the tactics of the enemy. Realize that excellence is a quality that is developed, something you will grow and mature in. Know that in the beginning, you may have to make a series of conscious decisions for excellence in order to reverse some old habits or thought patterns. I believe you can be excellent in everything you do and I know the Holy Spirit will help you!

Moving Along

1. Look back at the list of some of the characteristics of an excellent spirit. Which ones are you already exhibiting? Which ones can you grow in?

_____

_____

_____

_____

_____

2. In what ways have you not had an excellent spirit in the past? What tactics has the enemy used to keep you from being excellent? How can you begin to grow in excellence in the days to come?

_____

_____

_____

3. Ask the Holy Spirit to show you one area in your life today where you can take one step toward a more excellent spirit. What did He show you?

_____

_____

4. How does Colossians 3:17 instruct you to exercise an excellent spirit?

_____

_____

Stepping Stones

I have heard of you, that the Spirit of God is in you,
and that light and understanding and
excellent wisdom are found in you.
Daniel 5:14

And do not be conformed to this world, but be transformed by
the renewing of your mind, that you may prove what is that
good and acceptable and perfect will of God.
Romans 12:2

I will give you a new heart and put a new spirit within you;
I will take the heart of stone out of your flesh and
give you a heart of flesh.
Ezekiel 36:26

And this I pray, that your love may abound
still more and more in knowledge and all discernment,
that you may approve the things that are excellent,
that you may be sincere and without offense till the day of Christ....
Philippians 1:9, 10

And whatever you do in word or deed,
do all in the name of the Lord Jesus,
giving thanks to God the Father through Him.
Colossians 3:17

Mile Markers

• Your ability to receive the Word of God and allow it to work in your life depends on the condition of your heart.

• The wayside heart is arrogant and hard; the stony heart is shallow; the thorny heart is distracted and has its priorities out of order.

• Be diligent to develop and maintain good ground in your heart, so you can bear good fruit.

• You are a three-part being: spirit, soul and body.

• Your spirit is where communion with the Holy Spirit takes place. When you are born again, you have the ability to live from the inside out—from your spirit in obedience to the Holy Spirit, instead of according to your soul or your body.

• When the soul is healed and whole, heart attitudes can align with the Word.

• Having an excellent spirit does not mean aiming for perfection; it is a process that involves allowing the Holy Spirit to reveal His standards and His strategy to you and following through as though you are working for Him.

Travel Journal

Here's your opportunity to take a break, kick back and be creative as you express what the Holy Spirit has taught you about the attitudes of your heart.

P.S. The Holy Spirit works from the inside out!

SPIRITUAL WARFARE

Step 1: Realize that You Have an Enemy

Step 2: Recognize the Battle

Step 3: Use Your Weapons

Dear Fellow Traveler,

One of the most eye-opening revelations I have ever had was that there is more to life than the natural world. Oh, I had heard of heaven and hell—and I suppose I thought those two eternal destinations composed the entire spiritual realm. I did not realize that the spiritual realm also includes an active battleground on which war is being waged over the hearts and minds of people, over our decisions and relationships, over our circumstances and situations.

I first became aware of the spiritual war while I was in prison. It wasn't just the fact that I had to battle difficult circumstances because prison is a tough place. No, the spiritual conflict over my life started long before that. It was underway when I lived in an upscale Dallas neighborhood; it was raging while I was in college; it was even taking place when I was a child in the charming Kentucky town where I grew up. It's been going on over people's lives since satan was evicted from heaven centuries ago!

The forces of the kingdom of darkness and the forces of the Kingdom of light are warring over you right this minute. Among other things, the battle is over what you believe, over your ability to appropriate the power of God's Word, over receiving the love of the Father, over your relationship with the Holy Spirit, over your understanding of the Kingdom of God and over the fulfillment of His purpose for your life.

The Word of God will help you understand the spiritual war, teach you what your weapons are and instruct you in the ways of victory. It will also help you recognize your enemy and his tactics against you. Now, I am not encouraging you to focus excessively on the devil or look for demons around every corner. But it is important to be aware of your opponent and his methods, so you will know when he is trying to anger you, frustrate you, steal your peace, deny your destiny or bring oppression in some other way. It's impossible to resist an attack you don't recognize! I am not saying that resisting will prevent trouble or suffering in your life, but the Word of God teaches you how to use the weapons that have been given to you to stand against the enemy's schemes and overcome.

I want you to experience the victory Jesus has won for you—and I know you can. He longs for you to be equipped to fulfill your destiny and to be able to obliterate every obstacle before you. You are created with a God-given longing to be an overcomer, and part of your spiritual DNA as a believer is a desire to express the victory of the cross in your everyday life. You were made to live a life that reflects the nature of Jesus and advances His Kingdom in your sphere of influence. Understanding that you are in a war and knowing how to use your spiritual weapons will help you move forward in God's plans for your life, grow in intimacy with Him, untangle yourself from your past and bring greater depth and stability to your relationships. The more you can perceive what is going on in the spiritual realm, the better you can use your weapons and the more victory you are able to walk in.

God bless you as you live victoriously!
Mary

Step 1: Realize that You Have an Enemy

For this purpose the Son of God was manifested, that He might destroy the works of the devil.   1 John 3:8

His first recorded appearance is in the book of Genesis, when he enticed Eve with a piece of fruit. He brought devastation to Job's life, lured David into sin and even tempted Jesus Himself for forty days in the wilderness. He shows up again and again throughout the Scriptures, always with the wicked desire and fervent intent to separate people from God and bring destruction to their lives. Who is he? He is the enemy, otherwise known as satan or the devil. But he is not only a historical figure and the most evil character in the Bible, he is also alive and active today. He is not only "the" enemy; he is also *your* enemy.

Satan hates God, and he hates God's people. He is like a general who not only fights the battle, but also deploys his army of demons (also called evil spirits) to carry out his plans against believers and against God's Kingdom. He will do everything he can do to keep a person from being born again. Once people are born again, he will try to keep them miserable, frustrated, confused, angry and full of unbelief. He assigns demons to harass and oppress people with everything from discouragement to loneliness to financial trouble to the calculated and strategic breakdown of a marriage, a family, a business or a church. In fact, John 10:10 summarizes his battle plan: "The thief does not come except to steal, and to kill, and to destroy...."

John 10:10 summarizes his battle plan: "The thief does not come except to steal, and to kill, and to destroy...."

Just as there are many names for God throughout the Bible, there are also a number of names for the enemy. Just as the names of God reveal His character and His nature, the names of the enemy also expose his character, his nature and the ways he operates against us. Take a look at some of them.

- the enemy (see Matthew 13:39)
- satan (see 2 Corinthians 2:10, 11)
- the devil (see Matthew 4:1)
- the ruler of the demons (see Matthew 12:24)

- the wicked one (see Matthew 13:19, 38)
- the tempter (see Matthew 4:3)
- a liar (see John 8:44)
- the father of lies (see John 8:44)
- a lying spirit (see 1 Kings 22:22)
- a murderer (see John 8:44)
- the ruler of this world (see John 12:31)
- the prince of the power of the air (see Ephesians 2:2)
- the spirit who works in the sons of disobedience (see Ephesians 2:2)
- your adversary (see 1 Peter 5:8)
- the accuser of our brethren (see Revelation 12:10)
- an angel of light (see 2 Corinthians 11:14)
- the serpent (see Genesis 3:4, 14; 2 Corinthians 11:3)
- *Apollyon* (a Greek word which means "Destroyer") (see Revelation 9:11)
- A great, fiery red dragon (see Revelation 12:3)

As you can see, your enemy operates in a variety of ways; he is cunning, sly and determined to destroy you. But the good news is that Jesus is Lord! He is on your side, and His power is infinitely greater than the enemy's.

As we close this step, let me encourage you with the words Paul wrote to the believers in Rome, who, like you, found themselves the targets of the enemy's attempts to steal, kill and destroy. "And the God of peace will crush Satan under your feet shortly. The grace of our Lord Jesus Christ be with you. Amen" (Romans 16:20).

Moving Along

1. According to 1 John 3:8, for what purpose did Jesus come to earth?

_____

_____

2. According to John 10:10, what is the enemy's battle plan?

_____

_____

3. What do the following scriptures tell you about your enemy?

• Acts 5:3 _____

_____

• 2 Corinthians 4:4 _____

_____

• 1 Thessalonians 2:18 _____

_____

• 1 Peter 5:8 _____

_____

• Revelation 12:9 _____

_____

4. Fill in the blanks in Romans 16:20: "And the _____ of

_____ will _____ _____

under your feet shortly. The _____ of our Lord Jesus Christ be

with you. Amen."

Stepping Stones

The thief does not come except to steal, and to kill, and to destroy. I have come that they may have life, and that they may
have it more abundantly.
John 10:10

But I fear, lest somehow, as the serpent deceived Eve by his
craftiness, so your minds may be corrupted from the simplicity
that is in Christ.
2 Corinthians 11:3

Be sober, be vigilant;
because your adversary the devil walks about like a roaring lion,
seeking whom he may devour.
1 Peter 5:8

For this purpose the Son of God was manifested,
that He might destroy the works of the devil.
1 John 3:8

Step 2: Recognize the Battle

For we do not wrestle against flesh and blood, but against principalities, against powers, against the rulers of the darkness of this age, against spiritual hosts of wickedness in the heavenly places. Ephesians 6:12

In Luke 4:1-13, you will find a story in which the Holy Spirit led Jesus into the wilderness for forty days; while He was there, the devil tempted Him in a variety of ways. Of course, Jesus overcame every temptation, but I want you to see that even He had to resist the enemy. If the devil tempted Jesus, we can be sure he will oppose us too.

You can't the approach the enemy with an agreement that says: "I'll leave you alone if you'll leave me alone." There really is no neutral ground, and there is no avoiding the spiritual battle. When I write to you about this spiritual war, I am not only referring to the great cosmic conflict between good and evil, but also to the fact that the great conflict impacts your everyday life. The forces of evil seek to influence you in every way possible. The devil is not likely to appear on your doorstep

> There really is no neutral ground, and there is no avoiding the spiritual battle.

dressed in a red suit with horns on his head; he is far more crafty than that. Instead, he will try to influence you in subtle ways. For instance, a group of your friends may decide to go to lunch after church and not invite you—perhaps because none of them saw you at church that morning. The enemy can fire a thought at you to cause you to feel rejected and offended. Or he will try to lure you away from spending time in the Word by telling you that it won't make any difference. He may tell you, "Just one time won't hurt you." Or he may try to lead you into the trap of pride, judgment or comparison by whispering to you that you are more gifted, more attractive or more intelligent than someone else.

As a believer, you have victory over the enemy, but your ability to resist and overcome him starts with recognizing his activities against you. Remember, they will be subtle, and they will come against you in practical, everyday ways, such as:

- tension in a relationship, which may be the enemy's attempt to separate you from someone God has ordained you to be in a relationship with.
- the desire to give up on something the Lord has called you to do, which could be the enemy's tactic to keep you from moving forward in your destiny.
- feelings of unworthiness, which could be the enemy's attempt to keep you from growing in your prayer life.
- memories, thoughts, songs, smells or anything else that would ensnare you in your past, which can distract you from the present and discourage you about the future.
- a computer that keeps crashing, which could be hell's endeavor to cause you to lose your temper and speak unkindly to your coworkers or to dishonor someone in authority over you.
- a strategic attack on multiple fronts in an effort to steal the peace from your home. This could include a situation in which your potatoes are boiling over, the dog is barking, you look out the window and see your child falling off the swing, the phone is ringing, the delivery man shows up at the door, you trip over a toy and your other child walks into the room to show you how he can cut his own hair—all in a span of thirty seconds right before your husband gets home from work!
- the need for several unexpected major repairs in a short period of time, which could lead to financial stress or debt.

The enemy is quite clever, but once you begin to recognize his ways, you can resist him. Though warfare is a reality, the greater truth is that nothing touches your life that does not pass through the Father's hands, and He works all things together for good, according to His purpose (see Romans 8:28). You belong to Him, and when you do battle, you fight from a position of victory.

Moving Along

1. Fill in the blanks in Ephesians 6:12: "For we do not wrestle against

_____ and _____, but

against _____, against _____,

against _____ _____ of the _____

of _____ _____, against _____

_____ of _____ in the _____ _____."

2. Can you think of any situations, past or present, when you may have been in a spiritual battle and not realized it? What was it? Do you think you can better recognize a battle now? Ask the Holy Spirit to help you.

_____

_____

_____

3. Are you currently experiencing anything that could be the enemy's attempt to steal, kill or destroy something in your life? Describe this situation and the ways you can begin to resist the enemy.

_____

_____

_____

4. Have you ever been through a situation in which the enemy tried to cause damage or destruction, but God used it for good? What was it, and how did God work it for your benefit?

_____

_____

_____

Stepping Stones

And we know that all things work together for good
to those who love God, to those who are
the called according to His purpose.
Romans 8:28

Fight the good fight of faith....
1 Timothy 6:12

Be sober, be vigilant; because your adversary the devil walks
about like a roaring lion, seeking whom he may devour. Resist
him....
1 Peter 5:8, 9

For we do not wrestle against flesh and blood,
but against principalities, against powers,
against the rulers of the darkness of this age, against spiritual
hosts of wickedness in the heavenly places.
Ephesians 6:12

Step 3: Use Your Weapons

For though we walk in the flesh, we do not war according to the flesh. For the weapons of our warfare are not carnal but mighty in God.... 2 Corinthians 10:3, 4

Second Corinthians 10:3 says that even though "we walk in the flesh, we do not war according to the flesh;" and as you've already learned, Ephesians 6:12 tells us that "we do not wrestle against flesh and blood." What do these verses mean? Well, they mean that people are not your enemies. As believers, we are really fighting against the devil and his agents of darkness in the spiritual realm. Therefore, we must fight the spiritual battle with spiritual weapons.

We must fight the spiritual battle with spiritual weapons.

Below are seven spiritual weapons and instructions on how to use them.

1. *The Name of Jesus:* The Name of Jesus may be the most powerful word you can ever speak, because His Name carries all of His authority. As an example, let's say your child is being tormented by nightmares. Go into his or her room and pray aloud over that child in the Name of Jesus, and tell the child to say the Name of Jesus when he or she wakes up afraid. Thereby, spiritual authority is released into that situation.

2. *The blood of Jesus:* The blood of Jesus is one of the most powerful weapons God has given us for our protection, and it renders Satan impotent. Revelation 12:11 says that those whom the enemy violently opposes and accuses "overcame him by the blood of the Lamb." You too can overcome the enemy by the blood of the Lamb. For example, you can plead the blood of Jesus over your home, your family members, your possessions, your travel, or any area of your life in which you need the Lord's protection. To "plead" does not mean to beg; it simply means to appropriate the power of the blood by faith.

3. *The Word:* The Word is your primary weapon of truth. One of the enemy's most effective tactics is to subtly try to get people to believe lies, but the Word of God defeats the lies of the enemy. Like the Name of Jesus, God's Word carries God's authority. Next time the enemy tries to tell you something like, "God doesn't *really* love you," respond with the Word, answering aloud with a verse like, "God has loved me with an everlasting love, and He continues to draw me to Himself with lovingkindness" (see Jeremiah 31:3).

4. *Prayer:* True prayer is such a valuable weapon in the spiritual war. It is the way you receive God's strategy in a situation; it is the way you call heaven to your defense; it is the way to go on the offensive against the enemy; and it is the way you release the power of God into every circumstance. When you pray in the midst of a spiritual battle, you are like a soldier who approaches his Commander-in-Chief for the purpose of gaining strength, finding out how to win and being reminded that victory is sure.

5. *Praise and thanksgiving:* The enemy will do everything in his power to prevent you from praising and thanking the Lord. What he wants is for you to fall into grumbling, complaining and negative attitudes. He wants you to doubt God, but praise affirms your faith in God. There is always something for which you can be thankful, so no matter how difficult a situation may be, find something for which to praise and thank the Lord. For example, you may be so delayed when you are on your way to a meeting that you are late. But when you arrive at a certain intersection, you see an accident and realize that you could

easily have been involved in it if you had been on time. Instead of complaining about being late, you can praise God that He is ordering your steps, and thank Him for keeping you safe.

6. *Worship:* Worship is not just about music; it is about your priorities and what you value more than anything else. When you worship, however you worship, you are telling the Lord that He is your first priority, and you value Him above all else. The enemy opposes that, because he is always trying to get your focus off of the Lord. For example, if the enemy launches an attack against your finances, worship the Lord by continuing to give your tithes and offerings and maintaining a generous heart.

7. *Fasting:* Fasting is the intentional sacrifice of something (usually food, but also entertainment or something else you enjoy) in order to pursue the things of God, bring your soul into submission to your spirit, perceive His will, gain His strategy or see spiritual breakthrough. When you purposefully deny yourself something, you humble yourself, which puts you in a position to receive God's grace (see 1 Peter 5:5).

8. *The armor of God:* The armor of God, which you can read about in Ephesians 6:10-18, are defensive weapons that enable you to stand in the midst of the enemy's onslaught. Basically, putting on the armor of God means living according to the truth, living in the revelation that you are the righteousness of God, staying at peace, keeping your faith strong, being diligent to apply the provisions of your salvation and using the Word as a weapon.

I encourage you to learn to use your weapons and to rise up in the power of the Holy Spirit against the enemy. Never forget that you do fight from a position of victory, and the enemy's assaults against you are nothing more than the taunts of a defeated foe. The Lord has not only equipped you to fight; He's equipped you win.

Moving Along

1. As believers, who is our primary enemy? In which realm is our real battle?

_____

_____

2. Listed below are several scriptures pertaining to the spiritual weapons mentioned above. What does each verse teach you about these weapons? As you read these verses, ask the Holy Spirit to give you revelation about each of these spiritual weapons.

The Name of Jesus

Mark 16:17 _____

Philippians 2:10 _____

The blood of Jesus

Exodus 12:13 (the blood of the Passover lamb is a foreshadowing of the blood of Jesus)

_____

Revelation 12:11 _____

The Word

Psalm 119:105 _____

Psalm 119:161, 162 _____

Prayer

2 Samuel 22:4 _____

Jude 20, 21 _____

Praise and thanksgiving

Psalm 31:7, 8 _____

Psalm 149:5-9 _____

Worship

Psalm 119:164, 165 _____

2 Chronicles 20:21, 22 _____

Fasting

Isaiah 58:6-9 _____

Matthew 6:16-18 _____

The armor of God

Ephesians 6:10-18 _____

Romans 13:12 _____

3. Which weapon in the list above do you need to learn to use better?

_____

4. Using the list of scriptures above, choose one verse that corresponds to the weapon you want to wield better. Write it below, memorize it, begin to meditate on it and ask the Holy Spirit to show you how to practically apply it in your life.

_____

_____

_____

_____

Stepping Stones

For though we walk in the flesh,
we do not war according to the flesh.
For the weapons of our warfare are not carnal
but mighty in God
for pulling down strongholds, casting down arguments and
every high thing that exalts itself against
the knowledge of God, bringing every thought into captivity
to the obedience of Christ.
2 Corinthians 10:3-5

Having disarmed principalities and powers, He made a public
spectacle of them, triumphing over them in it.
Colossians 2:15

Therefore submit to God. Resist the devil
and he will flee from you.
Draw near to God and He will draw near to you....
James 4:7, 8a

You are of God, little children, and have overcome them,
because He who is in you is greater than he who is in the world.
1 John 4:4

Mile Markers

• Your enemy, the devil, is active today.

• The enemy will come against you in very subtle ways. His battle plan is to steal, to kill and to destroy.

• The enemy tempted Jesus in the wilderness, and he will oppose you too.

• Nothing touches you that has not passed through the Father's hands, and you war from a position of victory.

• Use your spiritual weapons, which include: the Name of Jesus and the blood of Jesus, the Word, prayer, praise and thanksgiving, worship, fasting and the armor of God.

• Using your spiritual weapons will help you gain and maintain victory in the spiritual war.

Travel Journal

Here's your opportunity to take a break, kick back and be creative as you express what the Holy Spirit has taught you about winning the spiritual war.

P.S. Corrie ten Boom said it best: "Jesus was Victor; Jesus is Victor; Jesus shall be Victor."

THE MIND

Step 1: Victory Begins in the Mind

Step 2: Use the "Philippians 4:8 Test"

Step 3: Abide in His Love

Dear Fellow Traveler,

Before I went to prison, I did so many ungodly things! But after I met the Holy Spirit and began to understand spiritual truth, I realized that my actions had all been conceived in my mind. For years, the enemy enslaved me and used me to accomplish his purposes—and he started by planting thoughts or ideas in my head. Just as I believe that "God works from the inside out," I know the devil does too—so be careful. He is actively destroying people and using their own thoughts to do it.

When the Holy Spirit began to help me in the arena of my mind, He did so by showing me that the enemy had twisted and tangled my thoughts for years. He revealed that the enemy is so crafty, he can imitate your own "voice" to the degree that you believe his thoughts are your thoughts!

For instance, you can be driving down the highway at 65 mph and think, *Yeah, that's the speed limit, but I can go 75*. Now you may consider ten miles per hour over the speed limit to be no big deal. But think about it: the enemy is the lawless one, and he wants you to break God's laws. Of course, he would start by causing you to disregard the laws of man, especially one that seems so easy to get away with breaking. If he can introduce, ever so discreetly, the idea that it's okay to disobey something like the speed limit, he can more easily draw you into other forms of disobedience later.

In the past, the enemy used the speed limit trick on me, but he also employed a host of other tactics to get me to cooperate with his plans. He influenced my thoughts so thoroughly and disguised them so effectively that he was able to manipulate almost every aspect of my life. I did not know the Word during that time, so I had no standard by which to measure my thoughts. I had never heard that I could resist my thoughts, so I just thought whatever popped into my head.

Has it ever occurred to you that all of your thoughts do not originate with you? Have you ever thought something and then wondered, *Where did that come from?* Well, it could have come from the enemy. That has certainly happened to me. For example, when I was assigned to work at the V.A. Hospital as part of the prison work-release program, I was not allowed to have a cell phone. But as soon as I heard that other inmates were breaking the rules of the program and getting cell phones, I thought, *I want a cell phone too!* Because following through on that desire would have been disobedient, I knew that desire was a thought planted by the enemy.

The Lord wants you to have victory in every area of your life. But in order to do so, you must begin to recognize the origin of your thoughts, desires, emotions and opinions. When the enemy is influencing your thoughts, he will lead you down the path of deceit, compromise, confusion, destruction and death. But when your thoughts are from the Holy Spirit, they will align with the Word, and you will be able walk in peace, freedom and confidence!

God bless you as you win the battle of the mind!
Mary

Step 1: Victory Begins in the Mind

Be sober, be vigilant; because your adversary the devil walks about like a roaring lion, seeking whom he may devour. 1 Peter 5:8

Now that you have gained a basic understanding of spiritual warfare from the previous leg of this journey, I'd like to focus on the fact that much of the battle begins in your mind. Remember, the enemy is sly and subtle, and he often gains access to your life through your thoughts and ideas—even the ones that seem harmless. I like to say that he'll send a mosquito to attack you before he shows up with a B-52 bomber!

For instance, let's say you are out shopping, and you see a friend. She waves to you, smiles, but does not stop to speak, even though you left a message on her answering machine yesterday. The enemy can take that situation and give you a thought such as: *I knew she didn't really like me*; or *She is so arrogant. She thinks she's too good to talk to me.* In reality, she may be a sweet, humble lady who thinks the world of you. There could have been all sorts of reasons she didn't stop to speak. Perhaps she was in a tremendous hurry on her way to an important meeting and had to stop at the mall to buy pantyhose; or, maybe she was rushing home to prepare dinner for guests. Even though, under similar circumstances, you might not have stopped to speak either, you find yourself offended by her behavior. If you do not recognize the scheme of the enemy, he can draw you into judgment (because you presume the woman thinks or feels something she doesn't) and then into anger and unforgiveness.

> Just as the battle begins in the mind, so does the victory. Every time you intercept the lies of the enemy with the truth of the Word, you quench a fiery dart.

See how easy that was for him? All he had to do was use a hurried friend who crossed your path that day, put thoughts in your mind to cause you to misinterpret her actions and motives—and bang! He has stolen your peace, caused you to be offended and tricked you into committing the sin of judging someone.

Just as the battle begins in the mind, so does the victory. Every time you intercept the lies of the enemy with the truth of the Word, you quench a fiery dart. This is one way you guard your thoughts. If you are anything like I was, this matter of guarding your "thought life" may be brand new to you and seem overwhelming. I don't catch every single thought the enemy shoots at me today, but I catch more than I did a year ago. A year from now, I want to be catching more than I do today.

Let me assure you, you can learn to deflect the arrows of the enemy before they take root in your mind, and to begin to unravel any tapestry of lies he has already woven into your thought patterns. Don't get discouraged because it will take time to grow in strength, endurance and accuracy of discernment as you resist the enemy. Here are a few suggestions to help you get started:

1. *Know the Word, and know it well.* The enemy will try to twist the Word and get you to think something that is not true. He will often attack you with a thought that is partly true, but partly untrue. Therefore, the better you know the Word, the better you can resist him.

2. *Be aware of your thoughts.* If you have never paid much attention to your thought life, start doing so. The more sensitive you become to what goes on in your mind and the more you know the Word, the more likely you will be able to stop a thought from the enemy at its onset.

3. *Remember, you don't have to agree with every thought that comes into your mind.* Decide that you are only going to agree with thoughts that align with the Word and reflect God's heart.

Moving Along

1. Can you see how the enemy can gain control of your actions if he can start by influencing your thoughts? How does Proverbs 23:7 affirm this?

_____

_____

_____

_____

2. How can knowing the Word help you stand against the attacks of the enemy?

_____

_____

_____

3. Take a moment and ask the Holy Spirit to help you guard your thoughts. Pray the prayer below or a similar one in your own words.

Holy Spirit, I need Your help to recognize thoughts from the enemy. Help me to resist every thought that will cause me to wander off the path of life on which You've put me. In Jesus' name, Amen.

4. What three Bible verses will help you specifically combat some of the lying thoughts the enemy is trying to get you to believe right now?

_____

_____

_____

Stepping Stones

The law of his God is in his heart; none of his steps shall slide.
Psalm 37:31

Commit your works to the Lord,
and your thoughts will be established.
Proverbs 16:3

Be sober, be vigilant; because your adversary the devil
roams about like a roaring lion, seeking whom he may devour.
1 Peter 5:8

For as he thinks in his heart, so is he. . . .
Proverbs 23:7a

Step 2: Use the "Philippians 4:8 Test"

Test all things; hold fast what is good. Abstain from every form of evil.
1 Thessalonians 5:21, 22

One of the ministers who has influenced me greatly is Joyce Meyer, and I especially like a phrase she uses often: "Think about what you're thinking about." Just as your physical body needs to be disciplined in terms of exercise, proper nutrition and rest, your mind also needs to be disciplined. An undisciplined mind is like an open battlefield on which the devil can attack from multiple angles, but a disciplined mind is like a well-guarded fortress.

In prison, when I first began to understand the need to discipline my thoughts and "think about what I was thinking about," the Holy Spirit gave me a simple, biblical filter through which to pass my thoughts. He showed me Philippians 4:8 and spoke to my heart that I needed to only think thoughts that fit into one of the categories in that verse. If a thought did not match one of them, I had to think about something that did! This strategy was extremely helpful, especially in the beginning when I was just learning about the enemy's desire and ability to impact my life through my thoughts.

An undisciplined mind is like an open battlefield on which the devil can attack from multiple angles, but a disciplined mind is like a well-guarded fortress.

Now I'd like to help you construct the same kind of filter in your mind. Take a look at this verse.

Finally, brethren, whatever things are true, whatever things are noble, whatever things are just, whatever things are pure, whatever things are lovely, whatever things are of good report, if there is any virtue and if there is anything praiseworthy—meditate on these things.
Philippians 4:8

As you can see, the eight categories that compose the "Philippians 4:8 test" are things that are: true, noble, just, pure, lovely, of good report, virtuous and praiseworthy. When I began to look at each of those qualities and tried to apply them to my practical, everyday thought life, here's the way I understood each one:

- *True.* When I tried to determine whether or not a thought was true, I first asked myself if it agreed with the Word of God. In addition, true thoughts are honest thoughts. There's no such thing as a "white lie," and there is no room for exaggeration.

- *Noble.* Noble thoughts are honorable and high-minded (in a good way!). Noble thoughts are not crass, petty or low. They are weighty, worthy, quality thoughts that have integrity and give honor to the Lord.

- *Just.* When I asked myself if a thought was just, I really asked myself, "Is this the right thing? Is this fair, impartial and free from judgment?"

- *Pure.* Thoughts that are pure are clean, holy, wholesome and untainted by the influence of the world and the enemy. Pure thoughts are without guile and free from deception.

- *Lovely.* I used to think about the most unpleasant things! But when I realized that I needed to think on things that were lovely, I had to replace those thoughts with thoughts that were pleasing, delightful, hopeful and not disturbing.

- *Of good report.* To think about things that are of good report really means to think about things that are excellent, positive, associated with goodness, have a good reputation, are well spoken of and respectable.

- *Virtuous.* Virtue is excellence. Virtues are "the good things," the positive aspects of a situation or the admirable qualities of a person. I also think of virtue as pertaining to high moral standards.

- *Praiseworthy.* To me, things that are praiseworthy are the things for which I can praise God. It's simple: anything that is worthy of thanking and praising God for is something you are allowed to think about!

I encourage you to ask the Holy Spirit to help you begin enforcing these categories in your mind because what you think about so significantly affects the condition of your heart. I also want to remind you that this will be a process. You may have had certain thoughts, thought patterns or mental strongholds for many years, and they are not likely to be broken overnight. But as your thought life aligns more and more with what God wants you to think about, you will walk in greater and greater victory. Ask the Holy Spirit to alert you any time you have a thought that does not fall into one of these categories. Dismiss the thought, and think about something that passes the Philippians 4:8 test!

Moving Along

1. Do you think about what you are thinking about? If your thoughts were projected on a big screen and everyone around you knew what you were thinking, how would you change your thoughts concerning one specific situation that is on your mind right now?

_____

_____

_____

_____

_____

2. What thoughts are you currently allowing into your mind that would be stopped when passed through the filter of Philippians 4:8?

_____

_____

_____

_____

3. What are the eight categories of the Philippians 4:8 test? List them and write one thought that fits into each category.

_____

_____

_____

_____

_____

_____

_____

Stepping Stones

The thoughts of the righteous are right, but the counsels
of the wicked are deceitful.
Proverbs 12:5

Casting down arguments and every high thing that exalts itself
against the knowledge of God, bringing every thought into
captivity to the obedience of Christ.
2 Corinthians 10:5

I will put My laws in their mind and
write them on their hearts;
and I will be their God, and they shall be My people.
Hebrews 8:10

Test all things; hold fast what is good.
Abstain from every form of evil.
1 Thessalonians 5:21, 22

Step 3: Abide in His Love

As the Father loved Me, I also have loved you; abide in My love. John 15:9

In addition to the Philippians 4:8 test, another grid that will really help you filter your thoughts is the love of God. When the enemy attacks your mind, one of his primary goals is to cause you to believe God doesn't really love you. He will attempt to steal your peace, cause confusion, make you suspicious and do all sorts of other damage, but those are not his ultimate goals. His ultimate goal is to convince you that God doesn't love you, that He isn't working for your good and that He is not on your side.

Because we know the enemy's intent, and we know he uses our thoughts as weapons to accomplish his purpose, we have to measure our thoughts against the unshakable truth that God loves us and guard against thoughts that try to persuade us otherwise. For example, if you get laid off at your job, your first thought might be, *How could God let this happen to me? I guess He doesn't really love me.* On the other hand, when you are abiding in His love, your first thought would be something like, *I know God has a good plan for me. I know He loves me, so this is all going to work out for good. He'll probably lead me to a better job.*

Can you see, from those two examples, that abiding in God's love really is a powerful and effective way to guard your mind? And what a change of perspective! We have to come to the point where we can quickly recognize and reject any thought that rises up against God's love for us. If a thought doesn't affirm His love and His heart toward you, know that it is a lie from the enemy, and don't let it linger in your brain.

My friend Helen has struggled so much in the area of her thought life, but she is learning to guard her mind. She told me one time, "Mary, if I had to boil down all the ways the enemy attacks my mind, it comes down to one thing he's always trying to get me to believe: God doesn't really love me."

I'll share with you what I shared with Helen. You've got to think differently about God's love toward you, and your thoughts have to align with His Word. The only way to get established in right thinking is to renew your mind by the truth of the Word. You see, Hebrews 4:12 says, "The Word of God is living and powerful, and sharper than any two-edged sword, piercing even to the division of soul and spirit, and of joints and marrow, and is a discerner of the thoughts and intents of the heart." The Word will help you guard your mind because it enables you to recognize thoughts that come from the enemy. When you can discern those thoughts, you can stand against them.

Remember, the enemy's ultimate goal is to make you think God doesn't love you. In order to guard against his schemes, find scriptures that communicate the love of God to your heart; memorize them, and

> We have to come to the point where we can quickly recognize and reject any thought that rises up against God's love for us.

meditate on them until you really believe them. That's what Romans 12:2 means when it says to be "transformed by the renewing of your mind." The more you are transformed, the stronger you become. And the stronger you are, the better you can guard your thoughts, resist the lies of the enemy and abide in the love of the Father.

Moving Along

1. What does Romans 8:38, 39 teach you about the love of God?

_____

_____

_____

2. The Scriptures below are all about God's love for you. Write each one, then choose one to memorize and meditate on.

- Jeremiah 31:3 _____

_____

- Romans 5:8 _____

_____

- Jeremiah 29:11 _____

_____

- 1 John 4:9, 10 _____

_____

_____

3. According to Hebrews 4:12, how can the Word of God help you abide in His love?

_____

_____

_____

4. Fill in the blanks in Romans 12:2. "And do not be _____ to

_____ _____ , but be _____ by the

_____ of _____ _____ ,

that you may prove what is that good and acceptable and perfect will of God."

Stepping Stones

For I am persuaded that neither death nor life,
nor angels nor principalities nor powers,
nor things present nor things to come, nor height nor depth,
nor any other created thing,
shall be able to separate us from the love of God
which is in Christ Jesus our Lord.
Romans 8:38, 39

And do not be conformed to this world, but be transformed
by the renewing of your mind, that you may prove what is that
good and acceptable and perfect will of God.
Romans 12:2

For the word of God is living and powerful,
and sharper than any two-edged sword, piercing even to the
division of soul and spirit, and of joints and marrow, and is a
discerner of the thoughts and intents of the heart.
Hebrews 4:12

As the Father loved Me, I also have loved you;
abide in My love.
John 15:9

Mile Markers

• Much of the spiritual battle begins in the mind—and so does the victory.

• The enemy is very strategic. He wants to control your actions and behavior, and he starts by influencing your thoughts.

• The key to defeating the lies the enemy tries to plant in your mind is to know the Word and use it as a means of quenching his fiery darts.

- Just as the body needs to be disciplined in order to function at its optimum, the mind needs to be disciplined as well.

- Use the "Philippians 4:8 test" as a filter through which to pass all of your thoughts.

- Measure your thoughts against the truth of God's love for you. If a thought refutes His love for you, it is from the enemy.

- The Word of God is like a sharp sword that can help you discern the voice and the work of the enemy.

Travel Journal

Here's your opportunity to take a break, kick back and be creative as you express what the Holy Spirit has taught you about the importance of your thought life.

P.S. Remember to "think about what you're thinking about!"

YOUR LOVE WALK

Step 1: Fully and Freely Forgive

Step 2: Be a Blessing

Step 3: Demonstrate the Fruit of the Spirit

Dear Fellow Traveler,

Along this journey, I have written to you of a life that is changed from the inside out, and on this leg, I want us to look at how you can express to others what the Lord has done in your life. I like to refer to this as your "love walk," which is simply the outward display of what He has accomplished, and is accomplishing, inside of you.

Once you begin to get established in God's love for you, you will find yourself wanting to express to others the love He has put in your heart. You'll find yourself eager to share the awesome things He's doing in your life with the people around you. The love inside of you will begin to overflow, and you'll start looking for ways to be an ambassador of His goodness everywhere you go.

When you are born again, the love of God springs to life inside of you, but your soul and your flesh will fight against your expressing it—at least that's what happened to me. The Holy Spirit did so much in my life so quickly while I was in prison. Among other things, He was healing me; He was setting me free; He was revealing the love of the Father to me; and He was bringing correction to a lifetime of wrong thinking. He was also teaching me to really love others in practical ways.

He used an especially needy, challenging woman in prison to help me learn to walk in love. For some reason, this woman annoyed me worse than anyone else—and she always turned up wherever I was. When I wanted to be alone in my cell, she showed up at my door. When I wanted to eat with friends in the chow hall, she would come and sit at our table. I couldn't seem to get away from her, so I did what any good Christian would do—I prayed and asked the Lord to get her out of my way! But He didn't. Instead, the Holy Spirit answered my prayer by showing me Romans 5:5, which says, "The love of God has been poured out in our hearts by the Holy Spirit ...."

What a revelation! I had not realized that God's love had been poured out in my heart, and that there was a well of love within me from which I had never drawn. I was waiting for the Lord to give me love for that woman instead of reaching down into my heart and accessing the love that was already there. I had the ability to love unconditionally—and didn't even know it! I simply had to exercise it.

The same is true for you. The Holy Spirit has poured out God's love in your heart, and you have the ability to love others—even, and *especially*, when it's not easy. The proof of your love for the Lord is your love for other people. The proof is in your sharing, your sacrifice, your selflessness and considering others before yourself. It includes forgiving quickly and completely, thinking the best of others, refraining from judgment, being patient and wanting the best for other people.

I encourage you to look for ways to share the love in your heart with everyone you meet!

God bless you as you spread His love!
Mary

Step 1: Fully and Freely Forgive

Even as Christ forgave you, so you also must do. Colossians 3:13

As I'm sure you can imagine, my going to prison was a difficult experience for my family. My parents handled it with tremendous grace and humility, but it was still painful. When the Holy Spirit began leading me to forgive the judge and the jury, and I began to experience the freedom that comes from forgiving and releasing other people, I told my parents what was happening to me. I can remember the day I called my mother and said, "Mom, I've really been working in my heart to forgive the judge and the jury and everyone involved in my case. Mom, please forgive them too. I don't want you to be *in* prison when I get *out!*"

If you have ever been deeply wounded or offended or had your life significantly affected by someone else's actions, your hurt or anger may have led you into the cell of unforgiveness. In *A Glimpse of Grace*, I wrote that "harboring unforgiveness is like drinking poison and hoping it will hurt someone else." That is true! It will also cause you to stay angry and keep you in a victim mentality. It will even hold you captive to your own sins, according to Matthew 6:14, 15, which says, "For if you forgive men their trespasses, your heavenly Father will also forgive you. But if you do not forgive men their trespasses, neither will your Father forgive your trespasses."

> Forgiveness is often the first step in your love walk, and there will be times in your life when it is the only step that will keep you moving forward.

You may wonder why I am writing to you about forgiveness in this chapter on love—because forgiveness is such a supreme expression of love. It requires you to put down your own rights, sacrifice your feelings and extend mercy to someone who has hurt or offended you, even in the most devastating ways. It is often the first step in your love walk, and there will be times in your life when it is the only step that will keep you moving forward.

Forgiveness is not a warm, fuzzy feeling; in fact, it has nothing at all to do with the way you feel. It is an intentional act of your will, a deliberate decision to not hold people accountable for the pain or trouble you have experienced as a result of what they said or did. It is a choice, not an emotion.

Once you have chosen to release the person or people who have hurt you, the next step in forgiveness is to begin to bless those you have forgiven. Ask the Lord to bless their lives, speak blessings over them (such as blessings of health and well-being, financial blessings, blessings on their family, blessings on their work, etc.). To speak a blessing over someone and mean it in your heart is to ask for God's best in his or her life. It may not be easy, but it is a powerful spiritual dynamic and a tremendous expression of love.

As you think about forgiveness, don't forget to forgive yourself. If you are like many people, you may be harder on yourself than you would ever be on others. You may be less gracious toward yourself than you are toward total strangers, as you impose standards that are higher and consequences that are more severe. If so, there may be some things for which you need to forgive yourself, and you know what they are. You can have a brand new beginning today, free from self-condemnation and self-inflicted punishment. Whatever you did or didn't do that has caused you to keep yourself in the bondage of unforgiveness, I urge you to release yourself right now. Choose to forgive yourself, quit beating yourself up and receive the grace and freedom Jesus offers you.

If we are really going to follow Jesus, then when we encounter things He encountered, we have to respond as He responded. Jesus had countless opportunities to forgive people, and He always did. That was just one expression of His love in action.

Moving Along

1. Have you ever put yourself in prison by not forgiving someone? When?

_____

_____

2. Is there anyone you need to forgive right now? (Don't forget about yourself.) Write down those names in the space provided, and then pray the prayer below or a similar one in your own words.

_____

_____

> *Father, I choose to forgive (<u>insert name</u>). Lord, I totally release (<u>him or her</u>), and I hold nothing against (<u>him or her</u>) anymore. I choose to bless (<u>him or her</u>). In Jesus' name, Amen.*

3. In your own words, why is forgiveness a critical step in your love walk?

_____

_____

_____

4. How is forgiveness an act of love?

_____

_____

_____

 Stepping Stones

But I say to you, love your enemies,
bless those who curse you,
do good to those who hate you,
and pray for those who spitefully use you and persecute you.
Matthew 5:44

And be kind to one another, tenderhearted,
forgiving one another,
even as God in Christ forgave you.
Ephesians 4:32

Beloved, if God so loved us,
we also ought to love one another.
1 John 4:11

Even as Christ forgave you, so you also must do.
Colossians 3:13

Step 2: Be a Blessing

Be kindly affectionate to one another with brotherly love, in honor giving preference to one another. Romans 12:10

It's easy to love in response to people who love you and treat you with affirmation and affection. It's not so easy to love when you encounter people who oppose you or when you find yourself in difficult situations with challenging people—but that's when love becomes love.

In this step, I want to encourage you to be proactive in your practical expressions of love and to be a blessing to the people around you. God is a giver; His nature is to bless, and as you grow in Him, you will continually develop aspects of His nature, such as compassion, mercy and a desire to help people. I hope you will begin to ask the Holy Spirit to show you how to be a blessing. He is so creative, and He knows what other people need, so He can give you the most amazing ideas about how to bless those around you—friend or foe.

In the leg about spiritual warfare, you learned that the enemy can resist you as you seek to follow the Lord. One of the forces that will oppose your desires and efforts to walk in love is your flesh. Your carnal tendency is to hoard, to cling to or to protect what you think is yours. It doesn't like to share, refuses to sacrifice and always demands its rights. But one of the best ways to walk intimately with the Lord and in His purpose is to overcome the flesh and walk in love.

> One of the best ways to walk intimately with the Lord and in His purpose is to overcome the flesh and walk in love.

Do you know that simply being kind is an expression of the love of God? I am convinced that our society is suffering from a severe lack of kindness and patience, and God's people have more ability than we realize to spread peace and joy in a variety of practical ways. Here are several suggestions you might want to consider as you seek to bless those around you.

- If you work in an office, refill the copier when the paper is low.
- Say "please" and "thank you" to retail clerks, bank tellers, restaurant servers and others who provide service to you.

- Be patient if you have to wait in line somewhere. Don't express impatience with body language, rolling your eyes or complaining. Let your words and expressions reflect grace, not frustration.
- Compliment people when appropriate, and do so honestly. Don't say you like a shirt or a tie if you don't; but if you do, let the wearer know.
- Celebrate occasions that are special to people—not just birthdays, weddings and babies, but a promotion at work, a significant achievement, a new house or a goal they've reached.
- If there is a coffee station at your workplace, don't take the last cup and expect the next person to make more coffee. Go ahead and make another pot before you walk away.
- Spend time with a person who is challenging to you. Sometimes all he or she needs is to know that someone cares.
- Pray for people.
- Offer to provide transportation for someone who is injured or disabled.
- Take a meal to people who are sick, have a new baby or have had a death in their family.
- When a public restroom counter has soap and puddles of water all over it, take a minute to wipe everything up. No one will know you did it, but it will provide a nicer environment for those who come in after you.
- Let the other person pick the restaurant.
- Keep granola bars (or something else edible) in your car for homeless people who may approach you.
- When you get good service in a store or a restaurant, let the manager know. Compliment the server by name.

Moving Along

1. Where do you spend the majority of your time during the day? How can you be a blessing to the people around you in that place?

_____

_____

_____

2. Think about the errands you need to run this week (the bank, dry cleaners, grocery store, etc.). Where can you express God's love through being kind? Ask the Holy Spirit to give you opportunities to do so.

_____

_____

3. What has God given you that you can give away? Is it joy? Is it an ability to bake so that you can give cakes or pies? Is it a desire to pray for people? Is it extra clothes in the closet? Is it the gift of being a good listener? List what He has given you and how those things can bless others.

_____

_____

_____

_____

4. What do the following scriptures teach you about being a blessing?
   • Romans 12:10 _____

   _____

   • Philippians 2:3 _____

   _____

   • Ephesians 4:32 _____

   _____

Stepping Stones

Therefore be imitators of God as dear children.
And walk in love, as Christ also has loved us
and given Himself for us, an offering and a sacrifice
to God for a sweet-smelling aroma.
Ephesians 5:1, 2

But if you love those who love you, what credit is that to you?

For even sinners love those who love them…

But love your enemies, do good, and lend, hoping for nothing in return;

and your reward will be great, and you will be sons of the Most High.

For He is kind to the unthankful and evil.

Therefore be merciful, just as your Father also is merciful.

Luke 6:32, 35, 36

Love never fails….

1 Corinthians 13:8

Beloved, let us love one another, for love is of God;

and everyone who loves is born of God and knows God.

1 John 4:7

Be kindly affectionate to one another with brotherly love,

in honor giving preference to one another.

Romans 12:10

Step 3: Demonstrate the Fruit of the Spirit

For a good tree does not bear bad fruit, nor does a bad tree bear good fruit. For every tree is known by its own fruit…. Luke 6:43, 44

One of the surest ways to walk in love is to walk in the Spirit. Now walking in the Spirit is the opposite of walking in the flesh. It will require attitudes and actions that are contrary to the world's way of doing things, but it leads to abundant life and victory. There is more to walking in the Spirit than simply exhibiting the fruit of the Spirit, but that is what I want us to focus on in this step.

> One of the surest ways to walk in love is to walk in the Spirit.

I like to encourage people to begin walking in the Spirit by cultivating the fruit of the Spirit in their lives. A common teaching, to which I subscribe, suggests that the primary fruit of the Spirit is love, and that the other qualities listed in Galatians 5:22, 23 are simply characteristics of love. So let's begin by looking at these verses.

> *But the fruit of the Spirit is love, joy, peace, longsuffering, kindness, goodness, faithfulness, gentleness, self-control. Against such there is no law.*
>
> Galatians 5:22, 23

You may be thinking, *Oh, I could never incorporate all of those things into my life! I've got a bad temper.* Or you may think, *I'm too hopeless to exhibit joy!* That's okay, because the Holy Spirit gives you the power to overcome those kinds of fleshly tendencies and has actually imparted the love of God to you. Therefore, it is possible for you to handle people and situations with:

- Joy
- Peace
- Longsuffering (or Patience)
- Kindness
- Goodness
- Faithfulness
- Gentleness
- Self-control

You always have a choice when it comes to how you are going to respond to any situation. You can choose to display the fruit of the Spirit or the "fruit of the flesh," which would be: pouting, fear, impatience, unkindness, mean-spiritedness, unfaithfulness or lack of loyalty, roughness and loss of self-control (which means letting your emotions or fleshly tendencies determine your attitudes or actions). When you walk in the fruit of the Spirit, you will usually know which

> Walking in the Spirit is not about "do's and don'ts"; it's about relationship.

specific facet of love is called for in a given situation. Sometimes you'll need to exercise more than one, and at times you may need the entire fruit basket!

When I find myself in a situation in which I don't know what to do or how to respond, I simply remind myself that I can yield to the fruit of the Spirit—and so can you. For

168

example, if you are frustrated, you can give way to patience. If you are confused or in an unnerving situation, you can yield to peace. If someone is rude to you, you can choose to allow kindness instead of offense to flow out of your heart. Because you can exhibit the fruit of the Spirit, you are never without a strategy or a resource in any situation. You can always be kind or gentle or patient.

When I studied what it means to walk in the Spirit, I learned that the Greek word for *walking* means, "to follow as a companion." That tells me that this matter of walking in the Spirit is not about "do's and don'ts"; it's about relationship. I've found that as our relationship with the Lord deepens, our tendency to express the fruit of the flesh diminishes. We become more inclined to walk in the fruit of the Spirit because we love Him, not because we are trying to perform for Him.

I pray, and I believe, that as you continue to walk more and more closely with the Holy Spirit, you'll also begin to increasingly express His love, and that you will keep maturing in the fruit of the Spirit.

Moving Along

1. List the fruit of the Spirit.

_____

_____

2. Fill in the blanks in Galatians 5:16, 17. "I say then: Walk in the _____,

and you shall not fulfill the lusts of the _____. For the flesh lusts

_____ the Spirit, and the Spirit against the _____; and these are

_____ to one another, so that you do not do the things that you wish."

3. Ask the Holy Spirit to highlight one specific fruit of the Spirit for you to focus on during the next week. Please write it below. Ask Him to put you in situations in which to demonstrate it as often as possible, and take advantage of the opportunities He gives you.

4. Take a moment and pray the prayer below or a similar one in your own words.

Lord, I really want to walk in the fruit of the Spirit. Please help me to be aware when I am on the verge of demonstrating the fruit of the flesh, and empower me to choose and exhibit the fruit of the Spirit instead. In Jesus' name, Amen.

Stepping Stones

Now hope does not disappoint,
because the love of God has been
poured out in our hearts by the Holy Spirit
who was given to us.
Romans 5:5

I say then: Walk in the Spirit,
and you shall not fulfill the lusts of the flesh.
For the flesh lusts against the Spirit,
and the Spirit against the flesh;
and these are contrary to one another,
so that you do not do the things that you wish.
Galatians 5:16, 17

For a good tree does not bear bad fruit,
nor does a bad tree bear good fruit.
For every tree is known by its own fruit.
Luke 6:43, 44

Mile Markers

• Forgiveness is often the first step in your love walk. At times, it will be the only step that keeps you moving forward.

• Holding unforgiveness in your heart is like drinking poison and hoping it will hurt someone else.

• It is essential that you forgive the people who have hurt you and that you also forgive yourself.

• One of the most practical ways to walk in love is to be a blessing to the people you come across in your everyday life.

• Simply being kind is one way to express God's love to others.

• The fruit of the Spirit is love, joy, peace, longsuffering, kindness, goodness, faithfulness, gentleness and self-control (see Galatians 5:22, 23).

• You demonstrate the fruit of the Spirit out of a loving relationship with the Lord, not out of legalism or a desire to perform. The fruit of the Spirit comes from intimacy with Him.

Travel Journal

Here's your opportunity to take a break, kick back and be creative as you express what the Holy Spirit has taught you about loving other people.

P.S. As the apostle John said, "Love one another."

CONTINUING THE JOURNEY

Step 1: Step Out, but Stay In

Step 2: Have Good Traveling Companions

Step 3: Walk On

Dear Fellow Traveler,

The Lord's heart for you, and for me, is that we grow up spiritually, keep becoming more and more like Jesus and never stop developing or being strengthened in Him. He wants us to be continually maturing in the Word, in our thinking, in our prayer lives, in our perspectives, in our relationship with Him, in every area of life. There is no final destination on the journey with the Lord; there is always another point of maturity, another level of intimacy, another degree of freedom and wholeness, another place of revelation and understanding. I like to say that the Lord keeps moving us to a new spiritual address, and it's always a move forward and a move up. Every time He relocates you, He'll help you get settled and show you that "you are here."

One of the things I have realized about this continuous process of spiritual growth is that the Lord does things in my heart—sometimes without my even knowing it—and then orchestrates a situation to show me what He's done. When I share this principle with others, I tell them, "Be on the lookout: God will give you a window of opportunity to see what He's done in your heart!"

This happens to me all the time. In fact, just the other day I went to the dry cleaners. When I arrived, a customer was being waited on, and I was next in line. Soon, several others were in line behind me. Suddenly, the door swung open and a woman bolted in, demanding her dry cleaning that instant. I could not believe it! She marched up to the counter and interrupted the lady who was speaking. When the clerk could not serve her right away, she walked behind the counter, screaming, "I'll just find my own clothes!" I felt totally invisible! But instead of being angry, as I would have years ago, I just watched in shock. Instead of being judgmental, I really felt sorry for her and thought, *Her whole life is probably uptight and in a hurry*—and I knew how miserable that could be! Instead of turning to the people behind me and saying, "Good grief, can you *believe* that woman?" I simply stood quietly and waited for the commotion to subside.

I was amazed when I realized that I had once behaved just as that woman did. I, too, at one time would have barged into a place of business, demanding immediate service with complete disregard for the other customers. What a window of opportunity to see not only how much the Holy Spirit had changed my responses, but to see again, with such gratitude, how much He had changed me.

Being changed really is the essence of your journey with the Lord, and it's a wonderful adventure. I am excited about the transformation He is working in your life! I believe He has accomplished so much in your heart as you have given your time and energy to walking the pages of this journey. Keep your eyes open for windows of opportunity to see what He's done in you. I'm sure you'll like what you see!

God bless you as you walk on,
Mary

Step 1: Step Out, but Stay In

The steps of a good man are ordered by the Lord, and He delights in his way.
Psalm 37:23

The continuation of a journey is just that—a continuation. You continue to make progress and to move from one place to the next; you keep stepping out as the Holy Spirit leads you. One of the biggest steps of progress I have ever taken was leaving prison, and I believe I learned some lessons then that may be helpful to you now.

Few people want to be in prison; most inmates despise being there and count the days until their release. The Holy Spirit did an amazing work in my heart one day when He led me to Psalm 16:6,

> Keep stepping out as the Holy Spirit leads you.

which says, "The boundary lines have fallen for me in pleasant places; surely I have a delightful inheritance" (NIV). When I read those words, I knew the Holy Spirit was saying to me, "Mary, just submit to the boundaries I've put on your life. In this season, they happen to be awfully tight. I want you to learn to stay within My borders not only in this season, but in every season to come. Walk right up to the boundary line, but don't try to push and live beyond it. I'll help you know the limits." Along with that revelation came the grace and determination to obey. To this day, every time I find myself in a new situation, one of the first questions I ask the Holy Spirit is, "What are Your parameters for this?"

Let me explain what I mean when I write about the boundaries the Holy Spirit sets. A friend recently quit her job to start her own business. Her former employer offered her an opportunity to keep working on a contract basis. Knowing that she was entering a new season of her life and that the new season would have new boundaries, she said to me, "Mary, I can't accept the offer to keep working for them as a contractor. The Holy Spirit is really impressing upon me the need to have the appropriate amount of distance from this company after I leave, and I believe this contract will keep me too closely connected to them as I go forward."

In my friend's case, the Holy Spirit's boundaries involved restructuring a professional relationship. As you consider the boundaries the Holy Spirit may set in your life, the following questions might help you get started.

- Do you need to make changes in the way you spend your time?
- What level of commitment are you supposed to make to people and projects?
- How long are you to be involved with an activity or situation?
- What new responsibilities are you to take on? Which responsibilities are you to release?
- Do you need to allocate your resources differently?
- What is your sphere of influence supposed to be?
- Where do you need to be geographically?
- In what areas of your life is the Holy Spirit giving you more liberty, and where is He placing restrictions or teaching you discipline?

As the Holy Spirit moves you to new levels of maturity or influence, or as He gives you new assignments, seek His boundaries and then stay within them.

The Lord has great things for you. Step out into them, but stay within His parameters. As you keep stepping out and staying in, you'll make tremendous progress on your journey!

Moving Along

1. Fill in the blanks in Psalm 16:5, 6 (NIV). "Lord, you have

_____ me my portion and my cup; you have made

my lot secure. The _____ _____

have fallen for me in _____ places; surely I have a delightful inheritance."

2. Are there any adjustments you need to make in order to observe the borders of the Lord in your life right now—either going farther or moving in? What are they?

_____

_____

_____

_____

3. Is the Holy Spirit asking you to step out into something new in the near future? If so, describe this new thing and ask Him what you can do to practically prepare for it.

_____

_____

_____

_____

Stepping Stones

Lord, you have assigned me my portion and my cup;
you have made my lot secure.
The boundary lines have fallen for me in pleasant places;
surely I have a delightful inheritance.
Psalm 16:5, 6 (NIV)

You enlarged my path under me;
so my feet did not slip.
Psalm 18:36

Cause me to know the way in which I should walk,
for I lift up my soul to You.
Psalm 143:8

The steps of a good man are ordered by the Lord,
and He delights in his way.
Psalm 37:23

And He has made from one blood every nation of men
to dwell on all the face of the earth,
and has determined their preappointed times
and the boundaries of their dwellings.
Acts 17:26

Step 2: Have Good Traveling Companions

I am a companion of all who fear You, and of those who keep your precepts.
Psalm 119:63

Good friends are such a treasure, and godly relationships provide joy for your journey, companionship along the way, a listening ear and words of wisdom and encouragement. The Lord's design is for people to be interactive and for us to both need and help one another. You were not created to travel alone. Nothing is more vital to your life than your relationship with the Lord. But that "vertical" relationship is both tested and enhanced by your "horizontal" relationships, the relationships you have with other people.

Many times, the Lord will use relationships as the settings in which to heal a broken heart, help you perceive your destiny or guide you as you make decisions.

Not only that, but nothing will cause you to get off track as quickly as the wrong relationships. Similarly, godly relationships will help you stay on the Lord's course.

> You were not created to travel alone.

As I've already shared with you, I was determined not to make any friends when I went to prison. I was only planning to stay about two weeks, so I saw no need to get to know anyone. But after the Holy Spirit began working in my life, He taught me a lesson I still apply: the Lord Himself will choose your friends. He will set the borders of your friendships, just as He establishes the boundaries in other areas of your life.

There will be some friends He asks you to walk closely with and others He will appoint as casual acquaintances. You may go through seasons when you have many friends, and times when you have only a few. The important thing is that you know who God has called you to walk with and what depth of friendship you are to have with each person. He knows what influences you need, what gifts you may have that someone else needs or what relationships and opportunities may come into your life through others.

As you walk with other people, you may encounter obstacles along the way. The enemy despises unity and strong, godly relationships. He will try to bring division, inflict hurt or offense, cause people to feel rejected, introduce conflict or cause miscommunication or misunderstanding. When you have a God-ordained friendship, contend for it. Many times, the greater the purposes of God for that relationship, the more intense warfare you will encounter. But let me assure you, a friendship that God has called you into is worth fighting for. Don't let the enemy thwart God's Kingdom purposes for that friendship any more than you will let him oppose or try to stop your personal destiny.

The people you walk with make a difference on your journey. Some will bring laughter and fun, some will be as "iron sharpening iron" (see Proverbs 27:17) and some will bring a combination of God-ordained challenge and encouragement. Whatever the Lord has in store as He gives you traveling companions, I really encourage you to keep your heart open for the Holy Spirit to choose and define your relationships.

> When you have a God-ordained friendship, contend for it. Many times, the greater the purposes of God for that relationship, the more intense warfare you will encounter.

Moving Along

1. Do you have good traveling companions? Who are they? Take a moment to thank the Lord for them. If you do not have such friends, ask the Lord to bring some into your life.

_____

_____

2. Are there any relationships in your life in which you believe you need to make an adjustment? Are there any from which you believe you need to make a gracious exit? Are there any you need to invest in and develop?

_____

_____

_____

3. Which traveling companions encourage you in your walk with the Lord?

- Who can you pray with? _____

- Who is as "iron sharpening iron" in your life? _____

- Who can you laugh and have fun with? _____

- Who can you call when you need to understand something in the Bible or a spiritual

  principle? _____

  _____

- Who can you turn to when you need wisdom or practical advice? _____

  _____

Choose one friend listed above and send that person a thank-you card.

Stepping Stones

As iron sharpens iron, so a man sharpens
the countenance of his friend.
Proverbs 27:17

He who walks with wise men will be wise,
but the companion of fools will be destroyed.
Proverbs 13:20

For where two or three are gathered in My name,
I am there in the midst of them.
Matthew 18:20

I am a companion of all who fear You,
and of those who keep your precepts.
Psalm 119:63

Step 3: Walk On

But you must continue in the things which you have learned and been assured of....
2 Timothy 3:14

One of the truths that is so critical to continuing your journey is to always remember that it is a journey. I've shared this before, but I want to encourage you again: you must keep walking. Your journey is a process of growth, which means you won't always get everything right. Keep walking anyway. Resist condemnation, refuse to give up, keep encouraging yourself and realize that the Lord is steadily moving you toward maturity in the way that best matches His heart for you.

It is so important to stay focused not only on where the Lord is taking you, but also on the process through which He leads you. It is also critical to celebrate your progress and growth, and one way to do that is to realize how far you've come.

> Your journey is a process of growth, which means you won't always get everything right. Keep walking anyway.

Focusing only on where you are going can cause you to get discouraged, but when you can glance back and see how many positive steps you've already taken, you can gain strength to go on.

I have a friend who is quite goal-oriented, and she often beats herself up when she feels she has fallen short. To encourage her, I often remind her of how far she's come by saying, "Just think, this disappointment would have emotionally debilitated you a year ago. Look how much stronger you are today, how well you are handling it and how quickly you can shake it off! Last year you would have pouted for two weeks!" That's what I mean by encouraging yourself and celebrating your progress.

As important as it is to celebrate how far you've come, it is equally crucial that you understand that your past can be one of the greatest hindrances to your moving forward. It is nearly impossible to walk into your future if you are shackled to your past. If you do not feel a lightness in your step and the freedom to march boldly into the next thing God has for you, then your past may have a grip on you. It may be trying to hold you back by reminding you of former failures or of broken dreams and disappointments. Jesus died to set you free from all of that, and the Holy Spirit is calling you into a wonderful and fulfilling destiny.

As you keep walking with Him, the Holy Spirit will periodically revisit some situations in which you believe you have already been established or some issues you thought were settled. This happens because the Lord often works in phases. Let's say you believe you have been set free from some sort of fear. You go along for several months, without struggling with that fear for the first time in years; but then one day, something happens, and you are suddenly afraid again. The Holy Spirit is simply showing you that it's time to move to a new level of wholeness and freedom. He is simply meeting you at every turn on your journey, giving you what you need at that point. The Holy Spirit is so committed to totally transforming you that He will deal with certain issues multiple times— and that's what it means to go "from glory to glory" (see 2 Corinthians 3:18).

> The Holy Spirit is so committed to totally transforming you that He will deal with certain issues multiple times—and that's what it means to go "from glory to glory."

Several years after my release from prison, I "beeped" as I walked through security in a Washington, D.C. airport. As I stepped aside to let the security officer wave the wand over me, my heart suddenly started racing, my palms began to perspire and my blood pressure seemed to soar. I felt the same way I did during the times I had been through security procedures and strip searches in prison. Even though I had been through airport security many times since my release, my response to that experience was different from all others. Later, I asked the Holy Spirit why I had been so affected by that seemingly routine event. He said, "Mary, it was just time to take your healing a little further. I was using your response to show that it's time for you to be healed in a deeper way." He was revisiting something He'd dealt with before, taking me to another "glory point."

Because the Holy Spirit works as I have just described, I encourage you to go through this workbook again in six months, and see what He will do then, which truths He will take deeper, what issues He wants to focus on at that time.

I encourage you to commit yourself to the process and to keep putting one spiritual foot in front of the other. You're on the greatest adventure of all time. As we close, I'd like to leave you with an exhortation for your journey, from Jude 24, 25:

> *Now to Him who is able to keep you from stumbling, and to present you*
> *faultless before the presence of His glory with exceeding joy, to God our*
> *Savior, who alone is wise, be glory and majesty, dominion and power,*
> *both now and forever. Amen.*

Moving Along

1. How do you normally respond when you encounter obstacles on your path? Knowing that God is calling you forward on the journey, how can you respond better?

_____

_____

_____

2. Think about a specific area of your life in which you have made progress as you've journeyed through this workbook. Maybe you are much more quick to forgive people now; maybe you are more consistent in your prayer life or more disciplined in your thinking. What is that area, and how have you recognized your progress?

_____

_____

3. Write Philippians 1:6, rephrasing it to make it personal.

_____

_____

_____

Stepping Stones

When he came and had seen the grace of God, he was glad,
and encouraged them all that with purpose of heart
they should continue with the Lord.
Acts 11:23

But we all, with unveiled face, beholding as in a mirror the
glory of the Lord, are being transformed into the same image
from glory to glory, just as by the Spirit of the Lord.
2 Corinthians 3:18

Being confident in this very thing, that He who has begun a
good work in you will complete it until the day of Jesus Christ.
Philippians 1:6

Looking unto Jesus, the author and finisher of our faith....
Hebrews 12:2

But you must continue in the things which you
have learned and been assured of....
2 Timothy 3:14

Mile Markers

• Step out into the new things God has for you, but always stay
within His boundaries.

• Don't overstep God's borders for your life, but walk all the way up
to the lines He has drawn.

• You were not made to walk alone. The Lord has handpicked traveling companions for
your journey.

• The Lord will choose your relationships and define the boundaries for them, just as He
does in other areas of your life.

• Keep walking on your journey. Don't get discouraged or be tempted to quit.

• Celebrate your progress by realizing how far you've come.

• The Holy Spirit often matures you in phases. Don't be surprised if He works on a
specific issue or area of your life more than once.

Travel Journal

Here's your opportunity to take a break, kick back and be creative as you express what the Holy Spirit has taught you about your continuing your journey with Him.

P.S. The Lord will give you windows of opportunity to see what He's done in your heart!

{ notes }